Words Their Way™

Letter and Picture Sorts for Emergent Spellers

Donald R. Bear
University of Nevada, Reno

Francine Johnston
University of North Carolina, Greensboro

Marcia Invernizzi
University of Virginia

Shane Templeton
University of Nevada, Reno

PEARSON

Merrill
Prentice Hall

Upper Saddle River, New Jersey
Columbus, Ohio

Library of Congress Cataloging in Publication Data

Bear, Donald R.
  Words their way : letter and picture sorts for emergent spellers / by Donald R. Bear, Francine Johnston, and Marcia Invernizzi.
    p. cm.
  ISBN 0-13-113591-0
    1. Word recognition. 2. Reading—Phonetic method. 3. English language—Orthography and spelling. I. Johnston, Francine R. II. Invernizzi, Marcia. III. Title.

LB1050.44.B433 2006
372.46¢2—dc22

2004053397

Vice President and Executive Publisher: Jeffery W. Johnston
Senior Editor: Linda Ashe Montgomery
Editorial Assistant: Laura Weaver
Development Editor: Hope Madden
Production Editor: Mary M. Irvin
Design Coordinator: Diane C. Lorenzo
Cover Designer: Ali Mohrman
Cover Image: Jean Claude Lejuene
Production Manager: Pamela D. Bennett
Director of Marketing: Ann Castel Davis
Marketing Manager: Darcy Betts Prybella
Marketing Coordinator: Tyra Poole

This book was set in Palatino by Carlisle Communications, Ltd. It was printed and bound by Phoenix Color Corporation. The cover was printed by Phoenix Color Corporation.

Pearson Education Ltd.
Pearson Education Singapore Pte. Ltd.
Pearson Education Canada, Ltd.
Pearson Education—Japan

Pearson Education Australia Pty. Limited
Pearson Education North Asia Ltd.
Pearson Educación de Mexico, S.A. de C.V.
Pearson Education Malaysia Pte. Ltd.

10 9 8 7 6
ISBN: 0-13-113591-0

Preface

Words Their Way: Letter and Picture Sorts for Emergent Spellers is intended to complement the text *Words Their Way: Word Study for Phonics, Vocabulary, and Spelling Instruction*. That core text provides a practical, research-based, and classroom-proven way to study words with students. This companion text expands and enriches that word study, specifically for emergent spellers.

Emergent spellers are just beginning to "write" on their own, using random marks, representational drawings, mock linear or letter-like writing, and random letters and numbers. To address the needs of emergent spellers, this text focuses on phonological awareness and vocabulary development as well as alphabet knowledge and concepts about print and initial letter-sound correspondences.

Words Their Way: Letter and Picture Sorts for Emergent Spellers provides teachers with prepared reproducible sorts and step-by-step directions to guide students through the sorting lessons. There are organizational tips as well as follow-up activities to extend the lesson through weekly routines. The materials provided in this text will complement the use of any existing phonics, spelling, and reading curricula.

More resources for word study in the emergent stage, including resources for using word study with students who speak Spanish, links to websites related to word study, and news about the *Words Their Way* CD-ROM and Video, other companion materials, and word study events can be found on the text's Companion Website. You can link to this site at

www.prenhall.com/bear

Contents

Overview

In this book, we present a sequence of activities for emergent word study and literacy instruction. Chapter 4 of *Words Their Way: Word Study for Phonics, Vocabulary, and Spelling Instruction* (Bear, Invernizzi, Templeton, & Johnston, 2004) describes word study for emergent learners in detail and suggests many activities to include with the sorts in this companion. Emergent spellers are found mostly in preschool, kindergarten, and the beginning of first grade. They cannot read in the conventional sense, but can follow along in simple predictable text with the support of memory and pictures, and it is from such pretend reading that they begin to develop a concept of word. They may not write at all or they might write with scribbles, letter-like forms, or random letters. If students are using letters to represent the initial sounds of words (spelling *cat* as K or *baby* as BB) they are moving into the early letter name–alphabetic stage, but will still benefit from many of the activities in this book. If they have a concept of word and are consistently representing beginning and ending consonant sounds, then they are no longer emergent spellers but letter name–alphabetic spellers and will benefit from the activities described for that stage in *Words Their Way* and the letter-name supplement.

ASSESSMENTS IN THE EMERGENT COMPANION

The first five sorts in this supplement incorporate assessments for all children in the emergent stage. These assessments indicate where students begin instruction. Other developmental assessments have been placed throughout the instructional sequence of this companion. The assessments in the final sort indicate what sorts and features to study next.

In a number of instances, benchmark scores are reported. These benchmarks are based on the *Phonological Awareness Literacy Screening for Kindergartners (PALS-K)* (Invernizzi, Meier, Swank, & Juel, 2002). Throughout this companion, we report benchmarks for spelling, concept of word, phonological awareness, and alphabet knowledge. These benchmark measures from PALS have been tested on a very large sampling of children and have been found to be reliable and valid (http://pals.virginia.edu).

WHERE TO BEGIN

The *Emergent Class Record* and the *Kindergarten Spelling Inventory* in Chapter 2 of *Words Their Way* are the assessments we use to determine the focus of word study instruction for students in preschool or kindergarten. The *Emergent Class Record* begins with random and letter-like scribbles and ends with short vowels. The *Kindergarten Spelling Inventory* is a 5-word list with a guide to interpret the spelling. Throughout this book we continue to refer to assessment tools that will help you make decisions about placement and pacing.

As noted, begin with the activities described in sorts 1–5 with all students because these sorts introduce essential sorting practices and activities, and students will learn through these sorts how word study is organized in your weekly schedule. The assessments that are spread throughout these first five sorts provide an understanding of students' literacy knowledge.

SEQUENCE OF INSTRUCTION

Emergent learners begin with concept sorts, and whenever possible, physical objects are used. Concept sorts with objects also become part of the daily routine. For example, when students wear winter overcoats, a few moments of the morning routine may be used to guide students to sort by color, material, hooding, or fastening. Similar sorts are conducted with the other concept sorts provided here and in *Words Their Way* and the *Words Their Way* CD-ROM.

Phonemic awareness, rhyming, syllabication, and sound play are studied in the second series of sorts. The third series of sorts focuses on alphabet knowledge and letter recognition. The fourth series of sorts focuses on concept of word in print, although attention is paid to this throughout the other sorts as well. Poems, jingles, and other short text selections are included to read with students and to use in word study activities throughout the study of beginning consonants. Once students have a stable concept of word, they begin to collect sight words they have learned to read in their familiar texts.

The fifth series of sorts introduces the systematic study of beginning consonants through explicit instruction using pictures. The sequence of instruction can be modified by teachers from that presented here to fit the sequence in their own core reading program. The last set of sorts in this supplement is a review and serves as an assessment of students' knowledge before going on to the letter name–alphabetic stage of word study.

PACING

Instruction in this supplement is set at an introductory and an average pace. There is a year of activities in this supplement, though most students will progress through these sorts in less than a year. Make adjustments in the pacing to assure that students master the sorts: If students catch on quickly, move to a faster pace, perhaps by spending fewer days on a series of activities or by skipping some altogether. On the other hand, pacing can be slowed by using additional activities when students need more practice. Chapters 2 and 4 of *Words Their Way* provide assessments, background information, more sorts and activities, organizational tips, games, and resources that are essential to organize your word study program for emergent readers and spellers.

ENGLISH LANGUAGE LEARNERS

Many teachers have students from diverse language backgrounds who are learning to read in English. Refer to Chapter 2 of *Words Their Way* as well as the Spanish word study program on the *Words Their Way* CD-ROM for a discussion of English language learning and differences in sound among languages. Throughout this book, possible confusions are noted for students who speak other languages.

MATERIALS

For each set of sorts there are *Notes for the Teacher* and suggestions to introduce and practice the sorts. We provide a variety of blackline reproducibles. There are sorts for students to cut apart to use over several days. There are also blacklines of reading selections that students can use for fingerpoint reading. Make your own copy of the reproducibles for teacher modeling in small groups or make transparencies to use when demonstrating on an overhead projector. The pages can also be enlarged to use in pocket chart sorts.

For independent or small group work, make copies of the handouts for each student, enlarging the original to eliminate the border and to increase the size of the words and pictures. Children can cut out their own set of sorts (developing fine motor skills in the process), but volunteers, parents, and cross-age tutors can help to prepare materials in advance to save instructional time. It will be apparent which young children will benefit from assistance in using scissors to cut up the sorts. Show them how to hold the scissors and the paper. After cutting out the pictures and using them for individual practice, the sorting pieces are stored in envelopes or plastic bags that have been labeled with children's names to sort again several times on other days or to take home.

Sorting and game templates and additional sorts are found in the appendix of *Words Their Way* and on the *Words Their Way* CD-ROM. Chapter 3 in *Words Their Way* includes additional ideas for managing picture sorts.

THE WORD STUDY LESSON

The four steps in a teacher-directed lesson are discussed in Chapter 3 of *Words Their Way* and in the *Words Their Way* Video. Take your time to introduce each of these four steps: *Demonstrate, Sort and Check, Reflect,* and *Extend.*

Demonstrate

Demonstrate the sorts and activities in small groups at a table, on the floor, on an overhead, or with a pocket chart. Read through the pictures with students, and have students say the names of the pictures with you aloud. Listen for the pictures that students know. The pictures can be used to extend children's vocabulary by talking briefly about new terms. However, do not make naming the pictures into a guessing game. Give the words as needed or eliminate unknown items from the sort.

Use the two or three key pictures at the top of each column to demonstrate the sort. Name the picture on a card and then check it with the key pictures. (Does *baby* go with *ball* or *monkey*? Listen, *baby–ball* or *baby–monkey*? I am going to put the picture of the baby underneath the picture of the ball because these two words sound alike at the beginning.)

Sort each picture in this way and place them underneath the key pictures. Go slowly as you demonstrate, and explain how pictures are alike or different. This explanation helps students learn specialized vocabulary that describes the categories; for example, *capital letters, sounds, rhyming,* and so on. Students sort by reading the pictures and words *aloud.* Saying the words together enhances student involvement, and the articulation provides essential information needed to sort by sound.

English language learners can participate in concept sorts easily by using equivalent terms from their native languages. The Spanish names for all of the pictures in *Words Their Way* can be found on the *Words Their Way* website. The *Words Their Way* CD-ROM has picture sorts to teach the sounds in Spanish.

Sort and Check

Students repeat the sort with you in small group time. Students can sort individually or with a partner, or they can contribute to a whole group sort. Pairing English-speaking children with English language learners will provide assistance with new vocabulary. Pull the key pictures out as headers for the sort. Have students set up their own key pictures in this way. Show students how to mix up the pictures and turn them face down in a deck. With a partner or in the group, students can take turns drawing a card and sorting pictures in the correct column. You can also pass out the pictures and have students take turns sorting their pictures for the group. To demonstrate how students are to check their sorts, sort a picture incorrectly. Show students how to recognize an error by naming the pictures in each column and moving the picture to the correct column. Finally, after checking a column, reflect by giving the reason(s) why you sorted the pictures the way you did. As you model a reflection, point to the pictures during the explanation, and English language learners can see how they can point out similarities when they explain their sorts.

Reflect

Bring the group together to have students reflect on why they sorted the way they did, or talk to individuals as you move around to check their work. Common phrases you can use in reflection are: *"These pictures are alike because . . . "* or *"I sorted these pictures in this column under the _____ because . . . . "* Because there are only so many ways to sort an easy sort, assure students that it is all right to say the same things that you or someone else did as long as it makes sense. Reflections can be made with partners, and they can be written down by the teacher and collected on a bulletin board or chart. As in most learning, children will need to see the reflection process modeled by the teacher. A reflection, for example, might be: *"I sorted these pictures underneath the picture of the cake because they all have the same sound at the end."* Emphasize the beginning sound by elongating it (*mmman*) or pausing briefly between the onset and rime (*c–ake*).

Extend–Repeated Practice Sorting

Students extend their experience with the sort in many ways. At the outset, students repeat the sort and then extend the sort by adding more examples, playing board games, and hunting for similar pictures. Over several days, students repeat these sorts in a group, for seatwork, with a partner, at centers, or for homework. Involve students in other routines described in *Words Their Way* for the emergent stage.

INTEGRATED WORD STUDY LESSONS

Daily literacy instruction blends brief lessons that occur throughout the day and are repeated over time. We plan a week-long routine that has students practice these essential activities to mastery. Within a lesson, there is a mix of activities in a number of essential areas: concept and vocabulary development, concept of word in print, literature phonological awareness, and alphabet knowledge and letter sounds. The teacher-directed lessons incorporate different components of this basic word study "diet" for the emergent learner.

In the *Words Their Way* Video, Mrs. Purcell demonstrates an integrated and efficient lesson with many of the teaching components essential for literacy instruction in the emergent stage. In Chapter 4 of *Words Their Way*, we discuss how Mrs. Purcell organizes instruction in a 20-minute daily block for an intervention program. The integration is illustrated in a sample lesson plan that comprises 60 minutes of a 90-minute literacy block that includes alphabet knowledge, phonemic segmentation, concept of word in print, and onset-rime discrimination. Such are the routines that are described in the sorts in this supplement for emergent learners.

Essential Literacy Activities in This Companion

Word study activities are integrated into these essential literacy activities: Read To, Read With, Write With, Word Study, and Talk With, or RRWWT.
The table below describes these essential activities.

Essential Literacy Activities	Procedures and Activities	Minutes
Word Study Phonological Awareness, Word and Letter Recognition, Initial Sound Correspondences, Concept and Language Development	*Word Study* includes picture sorts to teach beginning sounds; letter sorts and cards to teach the alphabet and letter recognition; concept sorts for thinking and vocabulary instruction; rhyming and syllabication activities; and language play with rhymes and songs.	10
Read To Concept, Vocabulary and Language Learning	*Read To* students from literature that offers rich oral language and that involves students in discussions as in Directed Listening-Thinking and Reading Activities (DL-TAs and DR-TAs). Vocabulary instruction has greater meaning when supported by what we read to students. Alphabet books for sound play are common Read To materials.	15
Read With Concept of Word in Print and Word Recognition	*Read With* students using the support of familiar, predictable, and rhyming texts. Students fingerpoint read to track brief and familiar texts on charts and in Personal Readers (see Chapter 5 in *Words Their Way*). Students match and arrange word cards and sentence strips.	10
Talk With Language and Vocabulary Learning	*Talk With* students to help their oral language grow. Creative dramatics, storytelling, and talking about meaningful things make it possible for vocabulary, language structures, and thinking to mature.	15
Write With Phonological Awareness, Initial Sound Correspondences, Verbal Expression, Concept and Language Development	*Write With* activities encourage students to analyze the speech stream. Students learn to segment words for individual letter-sound correspondences as the teacher models through think alouds and shares the pen.	10

Weekly Schedules In Emergent Word Study

Five days of word study can be divided into three segments: Day 1, Day 2, and Days 3–5. The first two days provide crucial and explicit instruction through teacher modeling and discussion. On Days 3–5, students work more independently, with repeated practice of the sorts. Given the integration discussed above, the Read With activities are introduced on Day 1 or Day 2, and this makes it possible to do word hunts and other word and letter recognition activities on Days 3–5.

Day 1
Read To: Literature Links
Read With: Concept of Word in Print
Demonstrate Sort
Talk With

Day 2
Repeat Sort
Check with a Partner
Reflect in Small Group
Extend at Seats or Centers
Read With: Concept of Word in Print
Letter and Word Hunts
Read To: Literature Links

Days 3–5
Repeated Practice with Sort
Extend Word Study at Seats, Centers, and Home
Read With: Concept of Word in Print
Read To: Literature Links
Write With

If you work with instructional groups, Day 1 can be staggered. In addition, Days 3–5 can be reduced and expanded. Most Read To activities can be presented in a larger group setting.

Word Study and Core Reading Programs

The activities in *Words Their Way* complement and expand activities in core reading programs. Each beginning consonant sound has its own set of pictures, and this will make it easier to use these picture sorts to support the curriculum in core reading programs.

    This is a remarkable period of literacy and language learning. The miracle of reading begins. We wish you the best in your teaching.

Donald Bear
Francine Johnston
Marcia Invernizzi

SORTS 1–5

Concept Sorts

NOTES FOR THE TEACHER

Begin your word study with sorts 1–5, as these concept sorts teach students how to sort, and include further assessments to guide the pacing of instruction in the rest of the sorts. Educators and parents may wonder why concept sorts are in a book on phonics, spelling, and vocabulary instruction. Concept sorts are designed for several purposes:

- Young children learn to categorize when they sort these pictures by concepts. They will use this cognitive skill later to sort or categorize sounds in phonics sorts.
- Concept sorts show students how to sort and to talk about their categories.
- Concept sorts advance students' vocabularies. Sorts provide support for English language learners as they acquire new vocabulary.

Concept sorts are the best place to show emergent learners the rudiments of sorting. Students learn how to organize a sort, how to read the pictures aloud, how to check one's work, and, finally, how to talk about the sorts. Even the youngest children can take part in these concept sorts, so everyone can participate without forming separate ability groups.

Concept sorts take advantage of the way we think in hierarchies. They are multifaceted and consist of a number of levels, parts, and subsorts, like a large tree with many branches. These concept sorts can be branched two or three ways. For example, in sort 1, the goal is to teach the rudiments of sorting, and we start with the most basic contrast: *those that fit and those that do not* (fruit / not a fruit). In the second fruit sort, students sort apples, bananas, and oranges into three columns. An optional layer of sorting in this case is to sort the pictures by characteristics (one piece of fruit, two pieces, cut pieces). In open sorts, students find additional categories for sorting.

A wonderful thing about concept sorts is that English language learners of all ages participate in concept sorts even without knowing the English terms because they can use their own language to identify the pictures. Older students learning English particularly enjoy the more complicated extended branching of concept sorts. For example, in the living and nonliving sort, students may be assigned to draw or find pictures of the next level of the sort; for example, one student could be in charge of finding birds and learning how to sort, classify, and categorize birds.

There are four other premade concept sorts on the *Words Their Way* CD-ROM: work and play, clothes and body parts, transportation, and creatures. In addition to these picture sorts, develop physical sorts for active learning. Many teachers have collections of objects, erasers, buttons, plastic animals, nuts and bolts, and so on, that can be sorted by various attributes. Possible physical object sorts are suggested in the sorts that follow here.

SORT 1   FRUIT CONCEPT PICTURE SORT

This first sort is the most basic of sorts and is easy to introduce. There are two sorts here: *Fruit / Not a Fruit* and *Apples, Bananas, and Oranges*. Integrated into this sort are several literacy assessment activities. Take your time and model carefully if this is your students' first sort.

Read To: Literature Links

Ehlert, L. (1989). *Eating the alphabet.* New York: Trumpet Club.
Freymann, S., & Elffers, J. (1999). *How are you peeling?* New York: Scholastic.
Lember, B. H. (1994). *A book of fruit.* New York: Ticknor & Fields.
Schuette, S. L. (2003). *An alphabet salad: Fruits and vegetables from A to Z.* Mankato, MN: Capstone Press.

Read With: Concept of Word in Print

There are three steps in a concept of word activity for emergent learners:

- Read the text together repeatedly so that children memorize the text,
- Track the text while reading, and ask children to track using their own copies,
- If children can track, locate words and collect words for a word bank.

The reading selections presented in this supplement are introduced in Read With activities when students begin to memorize at least one or two lines. These simple rhymes and jingles can be enlarged through overheads, made into handouts, written on chart paper, and posted around the room so that students refer to them often in word and letter hunts. We urge you to collect these familiar selections in personal readers as described in the activity section in Chapter 5 of *Words Their Way.* Learning to point accurately is a priority throughout the emergent stage, so children should have copies of text at their fingertips! Once students track accurately, they can collect sight words more easily, and add known sight words to their list of *Words I Read* described in sort 17.

Read the selection on page 21 titled *My Fruit* to your students. On a second reading, have students join in peeling, cutting, and washing motions while echoing the words. On subsequent readings model how you point to the words. Students may not know what it means to *peel* a piece of fruit or to *slice* a banana. Bring in real fruit to wash, peel, and cut up. Take time to introduce the vocabulary in this sort.

My Fruit

I peel, peel, peel my banana.
I cut, cut, cut my banana.
And I put the banana in a bowl.

I wash, wash, wash my apple.
I cut, cut, cut my apple.
And I put the apple in a bowl.

I peel, peel, peel my orange.
I cut, cut, cut my orange.
And I put the orange in a bowl.

PART I. FRUIT / NOT A FRUIT

Demonstrate, Sort, Check, and Reflect

Make a copy of the pictures on page 20 and cut them apart for sorting. Explain to your students, *"Here are some pictures to sort. Let's read them together."* Read through the pictures and explain that some of the pictures are fruits, and others are not fruits. Introduce the *apple* and the *hat* as key pictures: *"Here is a picture of an apple. An apple is a fruit and I am going to put it here at the top."* Hold up the picture of the hat. *"This is a picture of a _____? Hat, yes. A hat is not a fruit! What do you do with fruit? You EAT it. Would you eat a hat?"* (Children will enjoy the silliness of this idea). *"I am going to put the picture of the hat over here"* (to the right of the apple). *"Now, I am going to give you a picture to sort. Show us where your picture goes. If it is a picture of a fruit, put it underneath the picture of the apple. If it is not a fruit, put your picture underneath the hat."*

Next **demonstrate** how to **check**, **correct**, and **reflect**: *"When we are all done, we read our columns and check our work. Watch me, apple, orange, banana, apples, bananas, oranges. If we find one that does not belong we make a change."* Read through the non-fruit pictures to check and reflect on why you are sorting the way you are.

Sort Again with a Partner

Use prepared sorts, or have students work in pairs to cut up one sort to sort together. Remind students that *apple* and *hat* are the key pictures for sorting and should be put at the top of the columns. Pictures are stored in individual baggies after sorting.

Fruit	*Not a Fruit*
1 apple	**1 hat**
1 banana	comb
1 orange	ring
2 bananas	bat
2 apples	rain
2 oranges	map
cut apple	rake
cut banana	
cut orange	

PART II. APPLES, BANANAS, AND ORANGES AND ONES, TWOS, AND CUTS CONCEPT PICTURE SORTS

Ask students to sort again the same way they did yesterday, then explain that the pictures can be sorted another way. Pull out pictures of apples, bananas, and oranges to use as key pictures or headers and have students do the same thing. Tell them to sort the pictures under these new headers. A third sort can be done using the following key pictures: 1 banana, 2 bananas, and cut banana. Set up the headers and see if students can sort appropriately. Each of the sorts is shown below. Expect that changing the key pictures for sorting will pose problems for some students and be ready to model explicitly as needed.

Demonstrate

Demonstrate the sort using the key pictures from the fruit sort. Read the pictures with the students.

Apples	Bananas	Oranges		Ones	Twos	Cuts
apple	banana	orange		banana	2 bananas	cut banana
2 apples	2 bananas	2 oranges		apple	2 apples	cut apples
cut apples	cut banana	cut orange		orange	2 oranges	cut orange

Repeated Practice with Sorts: Fruit / Not a Fruit and Apples, Bananas, and Oranges Concept Picture Sorts

Conduct sorts in small groups until students can complete these on their own. Help students to reflect on why they sorted the way they did: *"These are fruits that I can eat and these are things that I would not eat. I sorted the fruit in this way: The fruits here beginning with the apple have one piece of fruit, the fruits in this column have two pieces of fruit, and the cut pieces are in this group."*

Read With

Reread *My Fruit*. Students fingerpoint read the first line of *My Fruit* using their own copies of the text. Model as needed for students who need assistance explaining how to track: "Put your finger on the title, *My Fruit*. Put your finger on the first line, *I peel, peel, peel my banana.*" Track the next line of text. Students fingerpoint read the same line of text on their individual copies. Recite and reread as often as possible: in the morning, in reading groups, independently, and to others at home. Listen for and use related vocabulary: *fruit, peel, seeds, rind, skin, sweet, sour, ripe.*

Talk With and Write With: Collect a One-Sentence Dictation

Familiar reading materials are created when you take dictations from students. Bring in a few pieces of fruit to taste. Fruits provide powerful experiences for student enjoyment and verbal interaction. In tasting and talking about favorite fruits, students produce the language for one-sentence dictations. "My favorite fruit" could be a topic to consider. To prompt a dictation you might say, *"What is your favorite fruit?"* As you take a dictation, write so that the child can see what you are doing. Say each word slowly as you write and talk about what you are doing: *"I will start with a capital letter here and end with a period."* As children develop letter sound knowledge, ask them to help you decide what letters to use: "What letter will I need to write the word *banana?*" After writing the sentence, read it back as you point to the words and ask the child if you got it right: "This says, *I like bananas.* Is that what you wanted to say?" Students can draw pictures to accompany their dictations. These dictations can be placed in their personal readers to reread regularly and use as a source for word hunts.

Letter and Word Hunts

Use the Read With materials and ask students to hunt for letters and words: "Let's find some words: Put your finger on the word *I*. Find the word *banana* at the end of this line." In letter hunts ask, "Find letters and words that you know. Find the letter *i* and the letter *p.*" Observe to find out what letters students know and how quickly they find them.

Extend

Extend with cutting and pasting fruit pictures from magazines. Students can be asked to bring pictures from home.

Include other fruit in a sort. A grape is another fruit you can use to introduce new vocabulary: Grapes come in *bunches* and have *stems.* Students can also hunt for foods with fruit in them: juices, desserts, and so on.

A song about fruit that children will enjoy is *Apples and Bananas* by Raffi. This song plays with sounds as the vowels in the words are changed ("*Epples and beneenees*"). Language play like this can enhance children's phonological awareness.

SORT 2   SHAPES: CIRCLES, TRIANGLES, AND SQUARES CONCEPT PICTURE SORT

Shapes and the language of shapes are basic to early childhood curriculum, and shapes lend themselves readily to sorting. We suggest starting with circles, triangles, and squares.

Read To: Literature Links

Burns, M. (1995). *The greedy triangle.* New York: Scholastic.
Carle, E. (1974). *My very first book of shapes.* New York: HarperCollins.
Dodds, D. A., & Lacome, J. (1999). *The shape of things.* Reading, MA: Scott Foresman.
Dotich, R. (1999). *What is round? and What is a triangle?* New York: Harper Festival.
Hoban, T. (1996). *Shapes, shapes, shapes.* New York: Harper Trophy.
Kaczman, J. (2001). *When a line bends . . . a shape begins.* Boston: Houghton Mifflin.

PART I: Demonstrate

Shapes: Circles, Triangles, and Squares

Make a copy of the pictures for sorting on page 22. Read through the pictures and listen for students who know the names of the shapes. Then pull out the picture of the circle, triangle, and square that are underlined and say, "*Here are three shapes to sort: circles, triangles, and squares. Let's look for other things that have these shapes.*" The final sort will look like this:

Part I. Shapes: Circles, Triangles, and Squares

circle	triangle	square
cookie	traffic sign	box
1 circle inside another	2 triangles	block
sun	1 triangle inside another	2 squares
2 circles	triangle bell	picture frame
		1 square within another

PART II: Demonstrate

Shapes: Circles, Triangles, and Squares

This second sort on page 23 is more complex and can be pursued once there is mastery of Part I. Students sort these shapes by their outline forms: dashes, stripes, shaded, and outlined shapes. The concepts and vocabulary (stripes, dashes) may be new to many students.

Part II. Shapes: Circles, Triangles, and Squares

dashed circle	**dashed triangle**	**dashed square**
striped circle	striped triangle	striped square
shaded circle	shaded triangle	shaded square
several shaded circles	several shaded triangles	several shaded squares
outlined circle	outlined triangle	outlined square

Students Sort and Check

Give each student a collection of pictures to sort in a small group sort. Continue to show students how to match the pictures they are sorting to the key pictures at the top. To check, begin with the key pictures and read down the columns. Explain: *"Let's read each column to check our sort."*

Reflect

Continue to model the language of reflection: *"How did we sort these pictures? These are all circles, these are triangles, and these are squares. These have four corners, these have three corners, and these have no corners."*

Talk With

By explaining as you sort, you'll use vocabulary that may be new to students. Key terms we use in this sort include: *corners, round, points, lines, angles, striped, shaded, outlined.*

English language learners may understand the English from their knowledge of other languages. For example, the English and Spanish terms are similar: *circle / circulo, triangle / triángulo, square / cuadrado (plaza), rectangle / rectángulo.*

Extend

Have students draw around the shapes with crayons. Listen to them talk as they color, and engage them in discussions about their favorite colors or the colors they are using. Do they know colors, shapes, and sizes? (Colors: red, yellow, green; shades of color: dark, light, bright; shapes: long, round, square, sharp.)

Add different shapes or different forms of these shapes, like triangles within triangles and circles within circles. Rectangles can be introduced.

Look for the shapes in your world. Draw pictures of these shapes, for example, a yield sign, a sun, a clock, or trucks. Cut and paste magazine pictures with these shapes.

Collect real objects that can be sorted on the basis of their shapes—books, dishes, puzzle pieces, blocks, and so on.

Read With: Concept of Word in Print

Prepare to read the selection on page 24 titled *Circles.* Make a transparency, create a chart, or place a paper copy in front so all can see. Also prepare a copy for each child. After reading the selection the first time, have students make shapes with large arm movements as you read it again.

Track one line of text at a time. Students can echo and fingerpoint read the same line of text on their individual copies. Model as students need assistance. "Put your finger on the title, *Circles.* Put your finger on the first line, *I make circles.*" Students should reread as many lines as possible, but focus on just one or two lines if they flounder on more. If students can point to the words, watch to see when they are thrown off by a two-syllable word (e.g., *circles*).

Circles

I make circles.
I make circles in the air.
I make circles on paper.
I make circles on the board.

Letter and Word Hunts

Ask students to look for letters: "Find the letter *m*." Make note of the letters that students know and how quickly they find them. You can also ask students to hunt for letters that have circles: *c, o, p, b,* and so on.

Students who can point with some accuracy can look for words: "Let's find some words: Put your finger on the word *circles*. Let's go to the next line. Put your finger on the word *I*. Find the next word, the word that begins with the *mmm* sound. *Mmmmake.*"

Alphabet Song: A, B, C, D, ...

Throughout the week, sing the alphabet song with students. Look for students who:

- know the song and handle *l, m, n, o, p* in punctuated fashion
- need the support of the group but can keep up with the group
- listen and learn the rhythm and a few phrases

In the next sort, students name the letters. We can use this sort to find out more about the students' alphabet knowledge.

Extend

Lay out a rope in the shape of the figures. Have students walk in small groups around the shapes. Discuss what they do at the corners.

The poem can be expanded for oral language development. *"How else can we make circles? I make circles _____."* (with a crayon, with paint, and with blocks). You can take a one-sentence dictation that begins, *"I make circles _____."*

SORT 3   ANIMALS, PLANTS, AND *ODDBALL* CONCEPT PICTURE SORT

This is a two-part sort. Interesting and complex questions arise when we define what an animal is. Do all animals have legs? Do all animals move? What are the differences between the land and water animals? What makes birds and insects fly?

Read To: Literature Links

There are hundreds of books that feature animals. Here are a few.

Campbell, R. (1982). *Dear zoo.* Salem, OR: Four Winds.
Christalow, E. (1999). *Five little monkeys jumping on the bed.* Boston: Clarion.
Hoban, T. (1985). *A children's zoo.* New York: Greenwillow.
Rey, H. R. (1941). *Curious George.* Boston: Houghton.
Walsh, M. (1996). *Do pigs have stripes?* Boston: Houghton.
Wells, R. (1998). *Old MacDonald.* New York: Scholastic.

PART I. ANIMAL / NOT AN ANIMAL

Demonstrate

Make a copy of the sort on page 25. Read the pictures with students. Part I is an animal / not an animal sort. Explain: *"Here is a picture of a horse. A horse is an animal. Let's look at the next picture, a tree. A tree is not an animal, so I am going to put the picture of the tree over here."* After the group sort have students sort their own copies of the sort independently or with a partner. Reflect by talking about attributes of animals (e.g., they move, they grow, they need food and water to live).

Animal	Not an animal
horse	tree (deciduous)
monkey	rope
rabbit	rock
turtle	wheat
dog	pine tree
whale	rose
bear	daisy
butterfly	grass
cat	cactus
bird	potted plant
worm	car
girl	
fish	

PART II. ANIMAL / PLANT / ODDBALL CONCEPT PICTURE SORT

Demonstrate, Sort, Check, and Reflect

Re-sort a plant / non-plant sort, using *horse* and *tree* as headers. Then show students how to subdivide the non-animal column into two columns: plants and *oddball* pictures, or pictures that do not fit. Pictures of the rock and the rope are part of the oddball column. *"Is a rope an animal? Is a rope a plant? I am going to put this picture to the side over here with other pictures that do not fit; they are not animals, or plants."*

On the second day have students repeat the sort and review why they sorted as they did. Ask them to look at the pictures under the tree and to find pictures that could be plants. Model how they will keep the plants under the tree. Ask them how plants are alike. Ask students to read the columns of their own sorts to check their work. See if students know the words in English and listen to how the names of these pictures are pronounced.

Animal	Plant	Oddball
horse	tree	rock
monkey	cactus	car
rabbit	wheat	rope
turtle	rose	
dog	daisy	
whale	grass	
bear	pine tree	
butterfly	potted plant	
cat		
bird		
worm		
girl		
fish		

Extend

Have students search through selected pages from magazines for pictures of animals and plants, then cut and paste the pictures onto one page. These pages can be displayed around the room.

If you have plastic or stuffed animals, students can sort them into categories of their choosing.

Talk With

There are many animals and plants, and there are many ways to describe the features of each animal and plant. You may find several other categories in students' discussions of these animals: how animals move (fly, swim, walk), where animals live (water, woods, farm, zoo), number of legs, indoor or outdoor plants or animals, useful to people or not, and so on. A sort for zoo animals and farm animals is described in *Words Their Way*.

Once these subcategories are established, additional examples will come to students' minds. For example, for flying animals, flies, pigeons, moths, and different types of birds may be added; and for water animals, there are different forms of fish, penguins, sea lions, dolphins, crabs, and sea stars.

Read With: Concept of Word in Print

The selection on page 26 is a three-line poem that invites movements. Prepare copies to use as you read it with the children. Ask three or four students to demonstrate movements for others to enjoy, clapping after each group performance. Students raise their voices with the excitement of jumping like monkeys. Point out the exclamation mark: *"An exclamation mark shows excitement."*

Animals

Birds fly in the air.
Fish swim in the water.
And monkeys jump everywhere!

Write With

Students enjoy dictating sentences about their favorite animals. You can ask students to include a color in their one-sentence dictations to create something like *Green crocodiles swim in the water*. Students can draw pictures to go with their dictations. Have students try to fingerpoint read their one-sentence dictations.

Sound Hunts

Choose a word from the Read With: *"Listen for words that begin with the same sound that you hear in _____. I am going to say two words. Do they have the same sound at the beginning?"* For example, *"birds – baby,* yes. *birds – table,* no." Emphasize the sound at the beginning of each word. Other frequently occurring consonants include *m* as in *monkeys, s* as in *swim,* and *f* as in *fish*.

Alphabet Knowledge

Use the Alphabetic Tracking Strip on page 60 for students to point individually. Keep singing the alphabet song regularly. Sing the song a second time and slow the singing down enough for you to point to large letters for students to identify, then observe to see who knows the letter name.

SORT 4   CLOTHES CONCEPT PICTURE SORT
Read To: Literature Links

Barrett, J. (1988). *Animals should definitely not wear clothing.* Aladdin Library.
Friedman, A. (1995). *A cloak for the dreamer.* New York: Scholastic.
London, J. (1989). *Froggy gets dressed.* New York: Viking.
Neitzel, S. (1989). *This is the jacket I wear in the snow.* New York: Greenwillow.
Peek, M. (1982). *Mary wore her red dress and Henry wore his green sneakers.* Boston: Clarion.
Taback, S. (1999). *Joseph had a little overcoat.* New York: Scholastic.
Wells, R. (1991). *Max's dragon shirt.* New York: Dial.

Demonstrate

Prepare a copy of the sort on page 27. Read the pictures with students. Select pictures of the hat, tie, shoes, coat, and gloves. Establish columns, pass out pictures to students, and model for them how to contribute to the sort: *"Is this something I put on my head? Something I put on my feet? Something I put over my body? Or something I put on my hands?"* The scarf may be an oddball category.

Here is how the sort will look:

Clothes Sort

head	feet	body	hands	oddball
cap	shoes	coat	gloves	scarf
stocking cap	work boots	sweater	mittens	
man's hat	tennis shoes	firefighter coat	dress gloves	
firefighter hat	boots	jacket	work gloves	
beret	slipper			
crown	skates			
lady's hat	sandals			
	socks			

Extend

This sort easily extends to physical object sorts such as coats. Try a "guess my category" sort with categories such as: shirts with buttons and without; short-sleeved shirts and long-sleeved shirts; shorts, long pants, and skirts; and so on. Ask children to move to an area of the room without telling them the category. See if they can figure out how everyone in a group is alike. We introduce button sorts as a part of our clothes sorting; see the buttons sort in Chapter 4 of *Words Their Way.* Shoe sorts are wonderful any season of the year!

Read With: Concept of Word in Print

The four-line selection on page 28 is easy to recite with movements and the single-syllable words will make it easy to track. Model and then have children track their own copies. Begin to assess concept of word in print among small groups of students. The behaviors discussed at the end of sort 5 include observing directionality and accurate pointing.

Socks, Shoes, Caps, and Gloves

I put socks over my toes.
I put shoes on my feet.
I put a cap on my head.
I put gloves on my hands.

Word Study to Accompany *Socks, Shoes, Caps, and Gloves*

There are several repeated beginning and final consonant sounds in this selection. Two words begin with /h/—*head* and *hands*. You may want to look for beginning and final /t/ in words like *toes*, *top*, and *put*.

The structure of this Read With makes it easy to create silly rhymes: *"I put a bed on my head. I put red on my head. I put a rubber band on my hand. I put sand on my hand."*

Talk With and Write With

Over and *on* are two prepositions in this story that can be elaborated upon with other activities: *"I put my shorts on, I put my sweater over my head, I put my scarf around my neck."* There are many activities with the hand and body. Young students like to draw around the shape of their hands with a crayon and then dictate a sentence like: *"My hand is big."*

Alphabet Recognition Assessment

Use the Alphabet Recognition Assessment on page 29 to assess students individually on capital letters. Tell students: *"Put your finger on each letter and say the name of the letter. Skip the letter if you do not know the name of the letter."* An assessment of lowercase letters is presented in the last sort in this supplement. Early emergent students will repeat the names of a few letters that they know. Late emergent learners will read the letters accurately at a faster pace.

Benchmarks: At the beginning of kindergarten, most students know the names of between 10 and 18 letters. At the end of kindergarten, students on average know the names of 20 of the 26 uppercase letters. Children who know more than 9 lowercase letters can be considered ready to study letter sounds.

SORT 5   FOODS CONCEPT PICTURE SORT – REVIEW AND ASSESSMENT

There are a number of assessments in this sort.

Read To: Literature Links

Prior to introducing this sort you can read about food using books such as those listed below. You can also assess children's participation in the Read Aloud activity with the questions that follow the first title. Similar questions can be used with the other books.

Sharmat, M. (1989). *Gregory, the terrible eater*. New York: Scholastic.

1. _____ Did the student look at you and the pages as you read?
2. _____ Did the student predict what Gregory would like?
3. _____ Did the student tell the differences between foods?
4. _____ Did the student recall items that Gregory liked or did not like?

Brown, M. (1991). *Sopa de piedras. Stone soup.* New York: Lectorum Publications.
    This story lends itself well to dramatization.
Carle, E. (1993). *Today is Monday.* New York: Scholastic.
Ehlert, L. (1989). *Eating the alphabet.* Orlando, FL: Harcourt.
Fleming, D. (1992). *Lunch.* New York: Holt.
Goldstone, B. (1964). *The beastly feast.* New York: Holt.
Hoban, R. (1964). *Bread and jam for Frances.* New York: Harper.
Soto, G. (1995). *Chato's kitchen.* New York: Putnam.

Introduce the Sort

Food sorts are complex because we have so many associations with food—when we eat it and how it is prepared. To assess students' knowledge of sorting, the concept of open sorts is introduced. In open sorts, students define the categories for sorting, and this is a window into their thinking.

Prepare the sort on page 30. Begin by reading through the pictures with the students. Note what pictures students can recognize and name, and for English language learners, what language they use to read the pictures.

Explain: *"Today, you will find your own way of sorting the pictures. Take the pictures you know, and sort them into three or four groups."* Have students explain why they sorted the way they did.

For students who are unable to get started, you may suggest groups in this way: *"If I put this picture with this one, can you guess why?"* For example, carrots and peas could be paired. Often this is enough to get them to find a third picture.

Food Sort: Breads, Beverages, Vegetables, Fruits Concept Picture Sort

bread	beverages	vegetables	fruit	oddball
taco	pitcher and glass	beans	apple	eggs
roll	tea or coffee	lettuce	banana	soup
pizza	soda bottle	carrots	cherries	
pancake	juice pack	tomatoes	watermelon	
	milk	potatoes	pineapple	
		peas	grapes	

Assess Concept Sorting

Assess students' engagement and understanding of the principles and procedures of sorting, using the questions that follow. Students who sort accurately and competently can begin to sort the same sorts for repeated practice at their seats or in centers.

Questions to Assess Students' Concept Sorts
1. _____ Did the student complete the sort?
2. _____ Did the student know the names of most of the pictures?
3. _____ Was the student able to explain the categories?
4. _____ Did the student develop an oddball category?
5. _____ Did the student develop categories other than breads, beverages, vegetables, and fruits?
    (foods for meals, foods that taste good)
6. _____ Did the student think of additional foods? (meats and prepared foods such as hamburgers)

Extend

Ask students to take away all pictures that are not fruits or vegetables: *"Leave your fruits and vegetables and take away all of the other pictures."* A discussion of the characteristics of fruits and vegetables can lead to language experiences with cutting and eating the fruits and vegetables. A number of sorts will come to students as they investigate the actual fruits: sorting by seeds, color, skin, ways we eat them, and so on.

Read With: Concept of Word in Print

Create text to reread by collecting one-sentence dictations. Begin by talking about your favorite food and then ask students about theirs. Everyone likes to talk about food, so this topic is easy to discuss. After oral sharing ask students to dictate a sentence about something that is meaningful and familiar about their favorite foods. The dictations can be written individually or on a chart. For individual dictations, write the sentence at the bottom of a page and have the student draw a picture to accompany the sentence.

My favorite food is _____.

For a group chart collect several sentences, using students' names to identify their ideas. Each of the students' dictations would begin as follows:

(Student's Name) said, "My favorite food is _____."

From Assessment to Instruction

A number of things have been accomplished in these first five sorts: Students have learned the fundamentals of sorting, they have been involved in essential literacy activities, and you have learned about their literacy development. All students will continue with the next group of sorts, the phonological awareness and rhyming sorts. But you may vary the pacing depending upon the needs of students.

SORT 1   Fruit/Not a Fruit Concept Picture Sort

Name _____   Date/Story Number_____

My Fruit

I peel, peel, peel my banana.

I cut, cut, cut my banana.

And I put the banana in a bowl.

I wash, wash, wash my apple.

I cut, cut, cut my apple.

And I put the apple in a bowl.

I peel, peel, peel my orange.

I cut, cut, cut my orange.

And I put the orange in a bowl.

Words Their Way: Letter and Picture Sorts for Emergent Spellers © 2006 by Prentice-Hall, Inc.

SORT 2   Part II. Shapes: Circles, Triangles, and Squares Concept Picture Sort

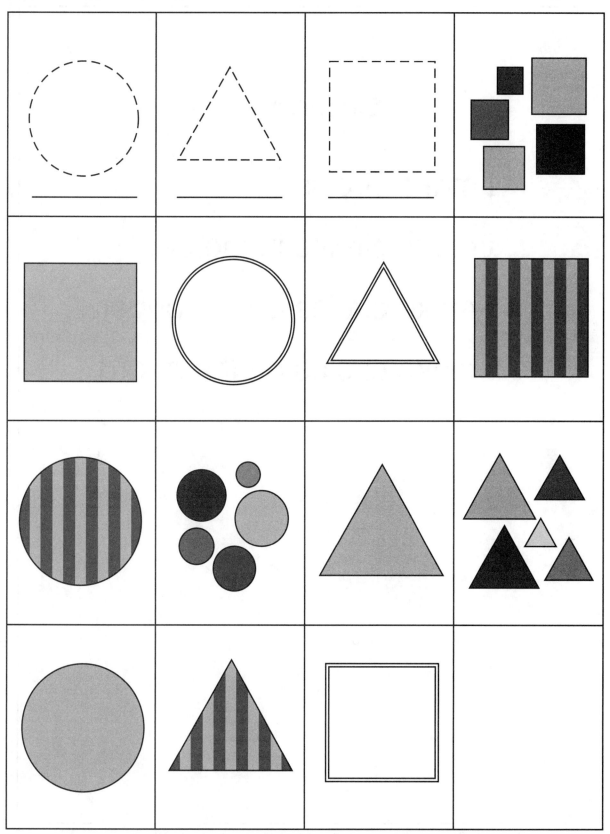

Name _____   Date/Story Number_____

Circles

I make circles.

I make circles in the air.

I make circles on the paper.

I make circles on the board.

Words Their Way: Letter and Picture Sorts for Emergent Spellers © 2006 by Prentice-Hall, Inc.

SORT 3   Part I. Animal/Not an Animal   Part II. Animal/Plant/Oddball

Name _____   Date/Story Number_____

Animals

Birds fly in the air.

Fish swim in the water.

And monkeys jump everywhere!

SORT 4   Clothes Concept Picture Sort

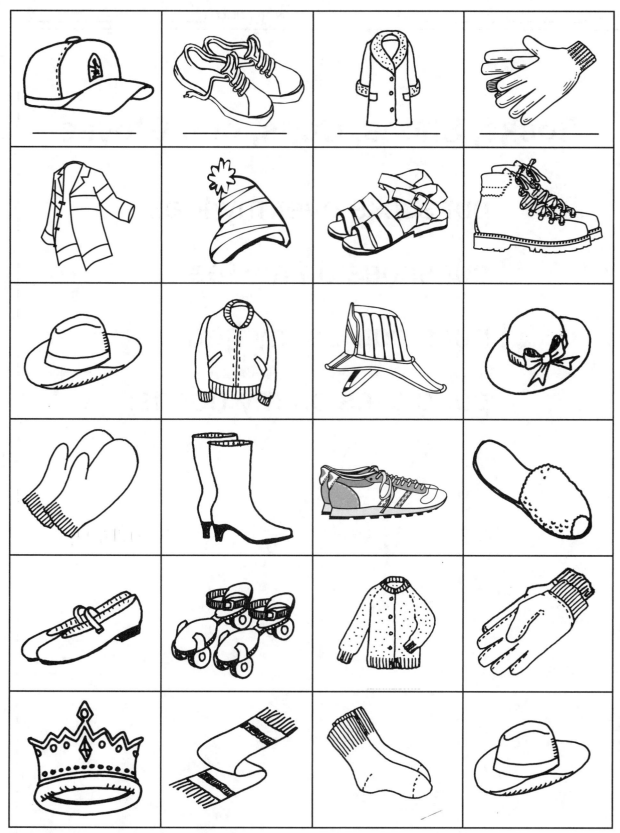

Name_____   Date/Story Number_____

Socks, Shoes, Caps, and Gloves

I put socks over my toes.

I put shoes on my feet.

I put a cap on my head.

I put gloves on my hands.

Name_____

Date_____

Correct_____

Words Their Way: Letter and Picture Sorts for Emergent Spellers © 2006 by Prentice-Hall, Inc.

SORT 5   Food Sort: Breads, Beverages, Vegetables, Fruits

SORTS 6-11

Phonological Awareness Picture Sorts

NOTES FOR THE TEACHER

In Chapter 4 of *Words Their Way* we describe phonological awareness as an umbrella term for a range of speech sounds that begins with rhyme and syllable awareness and advances to phonemic awareness, the ability to attend to, segment, or blend individual sounds within syllables. Teachers can direct children's attention to these sound units as they read to and with children, as they talk with children, and as they write with children. In this section we offer some lessons that focus on rhyme, syllables, and compound words. Phonemic awareness of beginning sounds is addressed in the sorts for initial consonants.

Children's literature is the starting point for many of these lessons. Emergent learners need to have their ears filled with lots of rhymes before they will be able to identify rhymes, match rhymes, or create their own rhymes. Fortunately, the literature of early childhood is filled with nursery rhymes, songs, and stories written in rhyme, so there is lots of material to choose from. We hope you can find the titles of books that we recommend, but if you cannot we hope that these lessons will serve as examples that will help you develop lessons based upon your own favorite books. With or without the books, the sorts can be used to engage children in active exploration of rhyme and syllables. To create your own word study sheets you may want to use the pictures in the appendix of *Words Their Way*. Chapter 4 in *Words Their Way* has more ideas for you to try and includes lists of resources.

Students' native language and dialects may lead them to pair words slightly differently. For example, students who speak Spanish may say that *rag* and *dog* rhyme. Ask students to read the pictures as they check, and this will give you a chance to hear if indeed they are said in the same manner. Specific differences among languages are described for each consonant beginning with sort 17.

WEEKLY ROUTINES FOR SORTS 6-11

Demonstrate, Sort, Check, and Extend

Each sort begins with an introductory demonstration. Activities are presented to extend the word study, and accompanying these activities are the Talk With, Read With, and Read To activities. Call students' attention to rhyming words, long words that can be divided into syllabic chunks, and compound words whenever you encounter them in the materials you read to and with your students.

Chapter 4 of *Words Their Way* has several rhyming sorts and activities that can incorporate the rhyming pictures and extend the rhyming sorts presented here: Matching and Sorting Rhyming Pictures, Inventing Rhymes, Using Songs to Develop a Sense of Rhyme and Alliteration, Rhyming Bingo, and Rhyming Concentration.

Draw and Label; Cut and Paste: Students can be asked to draw additional pictures that match or expand upon the sorts. The pictures from the blackline sort can be pasted into categories as a last step after the pictures have been sorted a number of times for practice.

Read With: Concept of Word in Print

Have students continue to reread the familiar selections introduced in these and in previous lessons. Many kindergartners and some first-graders will still need to practice tracking the words to learn concept of word in print.

Letter and Word Recognition

Students can be asked to identify letters and words in the texts. Students enjoy being the leader calling for classmates to find different letters and words. Students who have a concept of word in print will be able to find words they know and words that rhyme.

SORT 6   RHYMING PICTURE SORT:
OH, A-HUNTING WE WILL GO

Read To: Literature Link

Langstaff, J. (1991). *Oh, a-hunting we will go.* New York: Aladdin.

Oh, A-Hunting We Will Go is based on a traditional song available in a picture book adapted and illustrated by John Langstaff. It has a simple predictable rhyme that offers an easy introduction to matching rhyming pairs. The traditional song goes like this:

> *Oh, A-Hunting We Will Go*
>
> Oh, a-hunting we will go,
> A-hunting we will go.
> We'll catch a (fox)
> and put him in a (box)
> and then we'll let him go.

Various animals are substituted for the fox, such as a mouse who is put in a house and a bear who is put into long underwear. You may want to begin by teaching children the song. You can find copies of the traditional verses by searching the Web under the title of the song both with and without the word "Oh."

Use an overhead transparency of page 42 or copy the words onto a chart so children can see the words as they recite or sing. Children will be very successful at reading the book from memory with the support of the pictures. The sort below is based on the book, but could be used with just the words of the song if you do not have the book.

Read To, Talk With, and Read With

Introduce the book by looking at the cover and talking about the title. Talk about what the children might be hunting for. Read the book aloud, pausing to give children a chance to supply the rhyming words after the first few pages. Talk about the words that rhyme and go back through the book to name the rhyming pairs, using the pictures as clues. Read the book a second time and encourage the children to read along with you as you point to the words. Make the book available for children to read on their own and/or make a chart of the first five lines. We encourage you to make sentence strips of the lines for children to rebuild in a pocket chart and insert the pictures below in the blank spaces to change the verses. Children should be encouraged to fingerpoint read and reread the jingle to develop a concept of word.

Demonstrate the Sort

Prepare a copy of the rhyming picture sort on page 43 that features some of the animals and places where they can be put. (Enlarge the blackline master to maximize the size of the pictures and reduce cutting waste.) Model the sort by setting out all the pictures and selecting the *fox*. Explain: "Here is a picture of the fox. What word rhymes with *fox*? I am going to put the *fox* and the *box* together." Explain that *fox* and *box* rhyme because they end with the same sounds. Continue with each animal, pairing them up with the places in which they are put, in columns that will look like this:

box	**fox**
goat	boat
whale	pail
mouse	house
snake	cake
fish	dish

As a group name each pictured pair. Mix up the pictures and have the children sort under your direction. To make the sorting easier you can put together three pictures, two that rhyme and one that does not (e.g., *fox*, *dish*, and *box*), and ask a child to select the two that rhyme. This "odd man out" approach narrows the number of choices for children who are first learning to make rhyming matches. At this point children are switching from the concept sorts based upon meaning to rhyming sorts based upon sound. You can expect some confusion, so model carefully and explain why you are sorting as you do.

Sort, Check, and Reflect

Give each child a copy of their own pictures to cut apart and match for rhyming pairs. As you move around to check the children's work, encourage them to name the rhyming pairs. Ask them to tell you how the words in each pair are alike (e.g., they rhyme, they end with the same sound). Save the pictures to sort again over several days and to create the book described below.

Extend

Help children create their own books by pasting each rhyming pair from their sorting collection onto a copy of page 44 with the following frame sentence: "*We'll catch a _____ and put him in a _____ and then we'll let him go.*" Children can use their own invented spelling to fill in the blanks or you can do the writing for them.

Children should be encouraged to create their own verses using other animals. Some possibilities include: *Sheep in a jeep, moose in a caboose, frog on a log, cat or rat in a hat, bee in a tree, llamas in pajamas,* and so on. They can illustrate these and add them to their book.

Use the book or sentence strips to go on a letter hunt. Ask children to find particular letters in the text and point to them. "Who can find the letter *w*, the first letter in *we*?" Select words like *fox* and *box* as key words to develop a beginning sound sort as described in *Words Their Way*.

SORT 7 RHYMING PICTURE SORT WITH *HERE ARE MY HANDS*

Read To: Literature Link

Martin, B., & Archambault, J. (1987). *Here are my hands.* New York: Scholastic.

Read To and Talk With

The names for the parts of the human body are part of our basic vocabulary and are learned early on when we learn a language. Many books for young children feature body parts, but *Here are My Hands* (by Bill Martin and John Archambault) presents them in a simple rhyming format along with a multicultural cast of characters that makes the book especially appealing. Introduce the book by looking at the cover and talking about the title. Read the book aloud. On a second reading students may be able to supply the rhyming word if you pause after the first sentence of each rhyming set.

Demonstrate the Sort

Prepare a copy of the rhyming picture sort on page 46 that features body parts and display all the cut-out pictures. Begin by asking the students to help you find and name all the parts of a body. Explain that two of the body parts rhyme (*toes* and *nose*) and name the pictures to find them. Put *toes* under *nose*. Continue with *nose* by saying "What else rhymes with *nose*? Let's name the other pictures and listen for words that rhyme with *nose*." Find the hose and the rose and place them under *nose*. Repeat with the other body parts, involving the children as much as possible. The final sort will look something like this:

nose	knees	hair	head
toes	keys	bear	bed
hose	cheese	pear	bread
rose	trees	chair	

As a group, name the pictures in each column and talk about how they are alike — they all rhyme. Mix up the pictures and have the children sort under your direction. Use "odd man out" to support children who might struggle with finding a rhyme from so many choices.

Sort, Check, and Reflect

Give each child a copy of their own pictures to cut apart and sort, using the body parts for headers. As you move around to check the children's work encourage them to name the rhyming words. Ask them to tell you how the words in each pair are alike (e.g., they rhyme, they end with the same sound). Save the pictures to sort again over several days.

Extend

See if children can come up with words that rhyme with other body parts as you revisit the book or as children touch and name other parts of their body. You might play a game that goes like this: "Can you touch a part of your body that rhymes with *tears*? With *pin*?"

ears	tears
arm	farm

hand	band
eyes	cries
lip	zip
chin	pin
cheek	peek
neck	peck
wrist	list
feet	seat
hands	stands
leg	egg
knuckle	buckle

Read With

Many books and jingles on body parts are available to read with your children, and some of them are simple enough to be read from memory by emergent readers. On page 45 is a simple poem that can be written on a chart or prepared as a handout. Students enjoy reading this text to each other, directing others to follow the movements as they read. Students open and close their hands, eyes, and mouths several times as they read the last line. This is easy to read, and pointing to the only two-syllable word, *open*, will help students without a concept of word to learn to point accurately.

> *Open and Close*
>
> Hands open.
> Hands close.
>
> Eyes open.
> Eyes close.
>
> Mouths open.
> Mouths close.
>
> Open and close,
> Here we go.

Write With and Read With

There are many possibilities for writing with children as follow-ups. Have children brainstorm other things that they do with their hands or feet and record their dictations on a chart that can be reread together, starting with *"Here are my hands for . . . . "* Both hands and feet can be traced and cut out with students' ideas written on them by the teacher, or handprints and footprints can be used to illustrate their ideas.

Use a writing frame and encourage children to draw a picture in the space provided. You can also model segmenting the sounds, isolating a sound, and representing the sound with a letter as you write for them. Encourage the students to point to the words as they reread the sentences.

My _____ open. (eyes, hands, toes, mouth)

My _____ close.

SORT 8A, 8B, & 8C   "I CAN'T," SAID THE ANT
RHYMING PICTURE SORT

Read To: Literature Link

Cameron, P. (1961). "I can't," said the ant. New York: Scholastic. (Available as a big book)

In the picture book "I Can't," Said the Ant, ants and spiders work together to return a teapot to the kitchen counter after it falls to the floor. There are lots of rhyming pairs, and we offer you three different rhyming sorts to use with or without the book.

Read To and Talk With

Begin by reading the book aloud, pausing to give children a chance to supply the rhyming words cued by the picture. Be selective. Children will recognize many of the objects, but some, like *artichoke, trout,* and *thyme,* will not be familiar to most. Just supply those and keep going. On a second reading you may want to stop and talk with your children about some of these new words. The text for this book is too long and complicated to expect children to read along with you, but you can select three to five sentences to put on a chart or sentence strips along with a picture to cue the rhyme.

Demonstrate the Sort

The rhyming picture sorts we supply on pages 47, 48, and 49 begin with some of the kitchen objects cited in the book. Prepare the first set of pictures for modeling. Lay out *clock, fly, pie,* and *pan* for the children to see. Read aloud the sentence from the book that each came from, letting the children identify the rhyming word. Arrange these pictures in a row. Say, "*pie* and *fly*—those words rhyme. I am going to put the *pie* under the *fly* because they sound alike at the end." Move the pie under the fly. Put out the remaining pictures. Explain that there are more words that rhyme with each of these pictures. Model several and then sort the rest with student help. Leave the headers up and scramble the rest of the pictures. Give a picture to each child in the group to sort under the correct header. The sort will look something like this:

	8A	
clock	**fly**	**pan**
block	pie	van
rock	cry	can
sock	eye	man
lock	tie	fan

Sort, Check, and Reflect

Give each child a copy of their own pictures to cut apart and sort for rhyming pairs. As you move around to check the children's work, encourage them to name the rhyming words in each column. Ask them to tell you how the words are alike (e.g., they rhyme, they end with the same sound). Save the pictures to sort again over several days.

Extend

Introduce the other two rhyming sorts in the same way. Have the students sort them over several days. Try putting two and then three sets together for a grand rhyming sort.

	8B			8C		
bug	**mop**	**beet**	**jar**	**plate**	**bell**	**grape**
rug	top	feet	car	gate	well	tape
plug	shop	seat	star	skate	shell	cape
hug	pop	street				

Rhyming Bingo is available on the *Words Their Way* CD-ROM to print out and would make a good follow-up game. Rhyming Concentration, described in *WTW*, is also a good game to introduce here.

Brainstorm more rhyming words for each category. (These might include words like *smell* or *late* that cannot be pictured, but are high-frequency words that children would know.) You can also create sentences similar to the ones in the story. Here are some examples:

"What a bug," said the rug.
"Don't stare," said the chair.
"Use the mat," said the cat.
"Watch the log," said the dog.
"I've got to run," said the bun.

Children can glue the pictures that rhyme together. You might create a rhyming book for each child by folding several sheets of paper and gluing a different set of rhyming pictures on each page.

SORT 9A & 9B   RHYMING PICTURE SORTS WITH BRUCE MACMILLAN'S TERSE VERSE

Read To: Literature Link

McMillan, B. (1990). *One sun: A book of terse verse.* New York: Scholastic.

In *One Sun: A Book of Terse Verse* author and photographer Bruce McMillan creates the simplest of rhyme books using two-word "hink pinks" that describe a day at the beach. *Play Day* is a similar book by him, and either or both of these books can be used to introduce these rhyming sorts.

Read To and Talk With

Begin by reading the book aloud, pausing to give children a chance to supply the rhyming words cued by the picture when they are likely to be successful. On a second reading you may want to stop and talk with your children about any new words. The text for these books is so simple that children can easily pick it up and read it with the support of the pictures, the rhymes, and their memories, so leave the book out for children to use on their own.

Demonstrate Sort 9A

The rhyming picture sorts on page 50 feature some of the rhyming pairs from the books. Prepare a set of pictures for modeling and display all of the pictures. Challenge your students to find rhyming pairs. If they have difficulty, narrow the choices with the "odd man out" strategy. The pairs in this set are shown here.

sand	whale	bear	toe	duck	cub
hand	pail	chair	bow	truck	tub

Demonstrate Sort 9B

A second sort, on page 51, capitalizes on the many color rhymes featured in the two books. Make a copy of the sort and color in the spaces as indicated with crayons or markers. The pairs will be as shown here.

tan	man	pink	drink	white	kite
brown	crown	green	bean	blue	shoe

To prepare copies of this sort for your students to use independently you will need to do the coloring, or students can do coloring under your direction. Think of other color pairs like *red bed, yellow jello, black backpack,* or *gray day.*

Sort, Check, and Reflect

Give each child a copy of their own pictures to cut apart and sort for rhyming pairs. As you move around to check the children's work, encourage them to name the rhyming words.

Extend

Many teachers and children have created their own terse verse books using pictures that they have taken around the school building. Here are some possible hink pinks to find, create, photograph, and label. Can you picture them? You and your children can think of more.

ball hall or ball wall   eight date (on calendar)
scream team   bear chair   two drew   far car   new shoe   art cart
bright light   twin grin   grass class   school rule   sad lad   play clay

Feature children such as *Keith teeth, Hannah banana, Kim slim,* and so on.

Assessment for Rhyme

In the "odd man out" assessment on page 52 students have three pictures in each row and must underline or circle the two that rhyme. All of these rhymes have been featured in the sorts in this unit. Name the pictures for your students to be sure they are using the right labels and guide students in the completion of this assessment.

duck ball truck   bug rug cat
bear keys cheese   snake cake fish
bed bread sock   feet pan man
mop jar shop   clock rock fan
box bell shell   star cup car

SORT 10   SYLLABLES
Notes for the Teacher

Segmenting words into syllables is one aspect of phonological awareness that comes fairly easily to children. While rhymes and phonemes are abstract and depend on knowing what to pay attention to, syllables are concrete. We can physically sense syllables because each one is a separate pulse of air through the mouth. We can split words into syllables and leave clear spaces between them without distorting the sounds. Children can learn to tap them, clap them, or indicate them in other motoric ways that do not work readily for any other phonological elements. What children do not know is what those rhythmic units might be called and why we would want to pay attention to them. You can call them *beats, taps,* or *claps* but we see no reason to avoid calling them what they are—*syllables.* Draw children's attention to them when you read aloud and talk about them when you write for children. When you write for and with children, model how you can break a long word like *Saturday* into syllables before writing the letters for each sound.

Start With Children's Names

Write the name of each child in the class on pieces of tagboard. Write short names on short pieces about 3 × 4 and longer names on pieces about 3 × 10. Add a picture of the child if possible. Write the numerals 1–4 on tagboard and use them to create headers in a pocket chart. Select a two-syllable name like *Jose* and say it as you tap the card twice, once for each syllable. Explain to the children that there are two beats or two syllables in the name. Say the name again and have children clap the beats. Then put the name under the numeral two. Select a name with three syllables like *Amanda*, clap the syllables, and place it under the numeral three. Then select a one-syllable name. Continue to clap the syllables in everyone's name and sort them accordingly. After all the names are sorted, read down each column of names after saying something like, "*Let's read the names that have one syllable . . .* " Leave the names and key pictures in the pocket chart so that children can sort them again on their own. If you have digital pictures of the children you could create a master set by placing 12 to 20 pictures on a sheet of paper in a template. You will find many uses for these pictures, including giving each child a sheet to cut apart for sorting by syllables.

SORT 10A & 10B   HOW MANY SYLLABLES CAN YOU COUNT?

Read To: Literature Link

Carle, E. (1971). *The very hungry caterpillar*. New York: Scholastic.

Read To and Talk With

Read the book *The Very Hungry Caterpillar* (by Eric Carle) prior to doing this sort since it features many objects from the story. Introduce the book by looking at the cover and talking about the title. Read the book aloud, pausing to give children a chance to supply the words cued by the pictures. You might want to make sentence strips of the lines that feature the days of the week and the different foods he eats each day and put them into a pocket chart for Read With activities. Talk about any vocabulary (e.g., *plums*) that might be unfamiliar to the children.

Select some words from the story such as *hungry, caterpillar, very, butterfly, Monday, stomachache, Saturday*, and so on to model how the syllables in words can be separated as we talk and can be clapped or tapped. Say something like this, "Listen as I say this word: *hun – gry.*" Say it again as you clap along or tap your foot for each syllable. Invite the children to clap or tap along with you. Explain that words can be broken into syllables and continue to do this with several more words such as *beautiful, salami, cupcake, chocolate,* and *Sunday.*

Demonstrate Sort 10A

Prepare a copy of sort 10A on page 53, which features some of the one- and two-syllable words from the book. Model the sort by setting out all the pictures and putting the numerals as headers. Explain, "Here is an apple. Listen, *apple* has two syllables, *ap-ple.* Watch me clap (or tap) those syllables, *ap* (clap) *ple* (clap). I am going to put this picture under the number two because it has two syllables." Repeat with a one-syllable picture such as the plum, explain that it has only one syllable, and put it under the numeral one. Involve the children in sorting the rest of the pictures, clapping the syllables for each one. After sorting all of them, check the sort by reading all the one-syllable words and then the two-syllable words.

10A

1·	**2··**
plum	apple
leaf	sausage
pear	pickle
cheese	cupcake
pie	cherries

Sort, Check, and Reflect

Give each child a copy of their own pictures to cut apart and sort by the number of syllables. As you move around to check the children's work, encourage them to clap or tap the syllables. Ask them to tell you how the words in each column are alike. Save the pictures to sort again over several days and to create the book described below.

Demonstrate Sort 10B

On another day prepare a copy of sort 10B on page 54, which features some of the longer words from the book as well as some additional words. Identify any pictures you think your students might not know, such as *helicopter*. Demonstrate how to sort several words in a manner similar to the first sort before inviting the children to sort with you.

10B

3···	**4 ::**	**5 :·:**
butterfly	**caterpillar**	**refrigerator**
lollipop	watermelon	hippopotamus
banana	alligator	
hamburger	helicopter	
strawberry	motorcycle	

Extend

Combine the two-, three-, four-, and five-syllable pictures when students are sorting accurately and fluently. Ask the students if they can think of other ways to sort these pictures. They can separate the foods from the nonfoods, and can find the living things. Another sort can be things that grow and things that don't grow. Continue to look for words with two, three, and four syllables in other books and clap them. Children can look through magazines for pictures to add to their sorts.

Return to familiar readings to hunt for words by the number of syllables. Skip the single-syllable words and focus on two-, three-, and four-syllable words.

Use objects and pictures from concept sorts and categorize them by the number of syllables. The names of locations in your area such as streets, cities, schools, and states are a fine source of polysyllabic words.

SORT 11A & 11B   COMPOUND CUPCAKES

Notes for the Teacher

Phonological awareness includes an awareness of breaking and blending word parts that can be first explored in the creation of compound words. At this point it is not important for students to learn the term "compound word." Instead you can talk about putting two words together to make a big word or taking a big word apart. As children work with these words they also have the opportunity to refine or expand their vocabulary because meaning is explored as well.

Demonstrate

Cupcake is an easy compound word to introduce this sort. Make a copy of sort 11A on page 55 for modeling. Find the picture of the cup, the cake, and the cupcake. Hold up the cup in one hand and the cake in the other and name each, "Here is a *cup*. Here is a *cake*." Push the pictures together and add the picture of the cupcake. Explain, "When I put *cup* and *cake* together I have a new word, *cupcake*!" Continue to model how you put the rest of the words together. Then reverse the process. Hold up a picture of a compound word such as *skateboard* and say, "Can we say this as two words? *Skate board*. Let's find the two words that go together to make *skateboard*." Place the compound word first and then the skate and board pictures.

cup	cake	cupcake
dog	house	doghouse
foot	ball	football
snow	man	snowman
skate	board	skateboard

Sort, Check, and Reflect

Make a copy of the pictures for students to match up independently. As you go around to check students' work ask them to name the two pictures first and then the compound word that they form. Remember, do not expect emergent readers to tell you that these are compound words.

Extend

A second set of pictures (sort 11B on page 56) is included to use for another lesson. When students are facile at sort 11B, combine it with sort 11A. The second set is as follows:

lip	stick	lipstick
finger	nail	fingernail
sun	glasses	sunglasses
rain	coat	raincoat
mail	box	mailbox

Repeat this activity orally by saying the following words and asking students to say the words that make up the compound. Reverse the process by saying the individual words and asking students to say the compound word. Children might be asked to choose a word and illustrate it. You can pose riddles such as, "I am thinking of a word that has *sand* and *box*." Clap the syllables in the larger words like *pocketbook, newspaper, basketball,* and so on. Here are some more compound words made up of concrete word parts. Children might draw their own pictures to illustrate some of these.

lighthouse	sandbox	basketball
pocketbook	cowboy	hairbrush
starfish	fireman	pigpen
pancake	goldfish	popcorn
butterfly	doorbell	treetop
handbag	ladybug	rainbow

Name _____   Date/Story Number_____

Oh, A-Hunting We Will Go

Oh, a-hunting we will go,

A-hunting we will go.

We'll catch a _____

and put him in a _____

and then we'll let him go.

Frame sentences for cut-and-paste book

Name _____   Date/Story Number_____

We'll catch a _____
and put him in a _____
and then we'll let him go.

We'll catch a _____
and put him in a _____
and then we'll let him go.

Name _____   Date/Story Number_____

Open and Close

Hands open.
Hands close.

Eyes open.
Eyes close.

Mouths open.
Mouths close.

Open and close,
Here we go.

Words Their Way: Letter and Picture Sorts for Emergent Spellers © 2006 by Prentice-Hall, Inc.

Words Their Way: Letter and Picture Sorts for Emergent Spellers © 2006 by Prentice-Hall, Inc.

SORT 8A   Rhyming Sort for *"I Can't," Said the Ant*

Rhyming Sort for *"I Can't," Said the Ant*

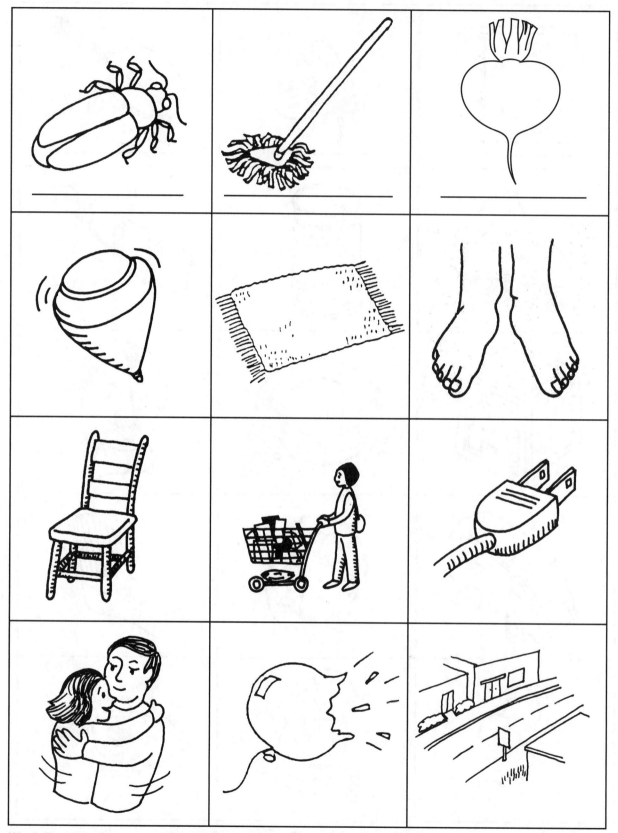

Words Their Way: Letter and Picture Sorts for Emergent Spellers © 2006 by Prentice-Hall, Inc.

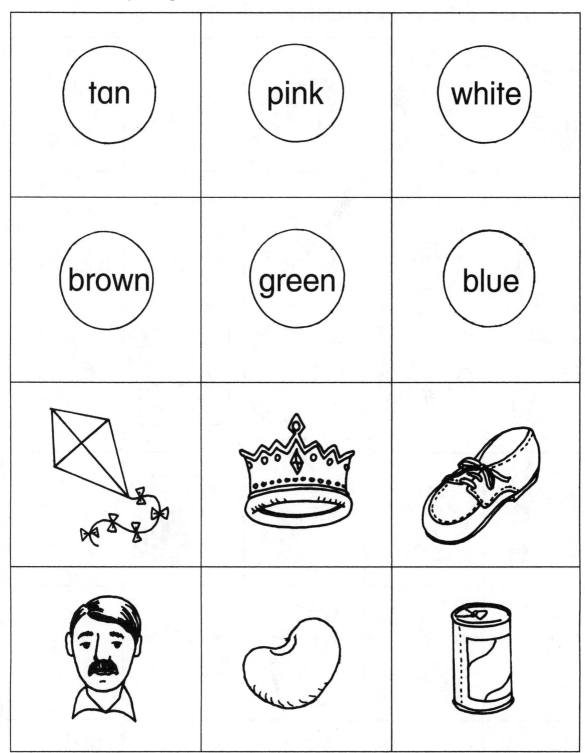

SORT 9   Assessment for Rhyme
Instructions: Circle the two pictures that rhyme.

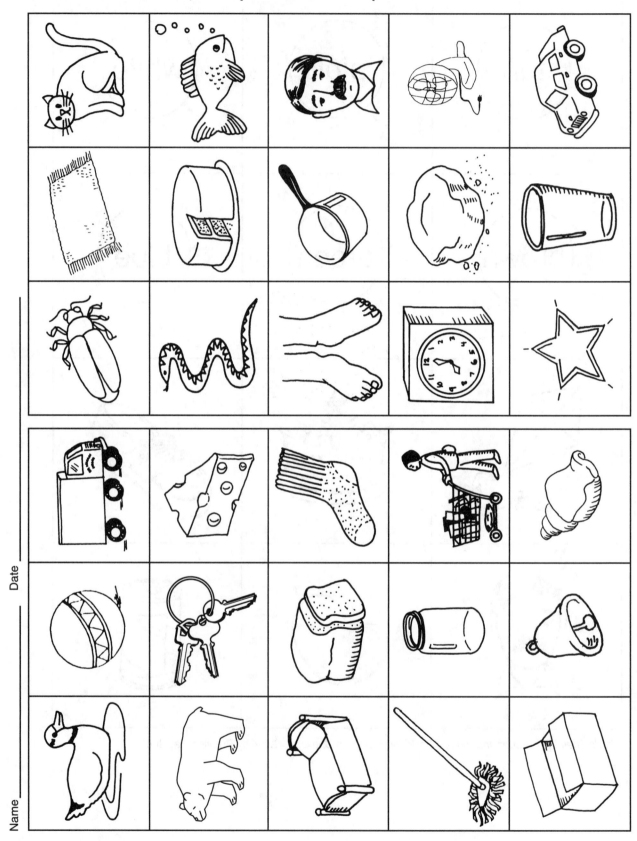

Words Their Way: Letter and Picture Sorts for Emergent Spellers © 2006 by Prentice-Hall, Inc.

Name

Date

SORT 10A   How Many Syllables Can You Count?

SORT 10B   How Many Syllables Can You Count?

SORT 11A   Compound Words

SORT 11B   Compound Words

SORTS 12-14

Alphabet Knowledge

NOTES FOR THE TEACHER

There is much to learn about the alphabet, and activities are suggested throughout this book. In this section we offer an alphabet tracking strip and some sorts that compare capital and lowercase letters across a variety of font styles.

Earlier we recommended that students sing the alphabet song and identify letters as you call them out. Before beginning the sorts in this section we recommend that you assess students' alphabet knowledge to see who will need extensive work on the alphabet. Assessment should include singing the alphabet song, reciting the letters while pointing to them, and identifying them in random order (both uppercase and lowercase). Students also need to be able to produce the letters, and you might add this for students who do well with the other assessments. Once we know that students can recite the alphabet, at least through song and pointing, we look at more complicated activities, like finding letters within the alphabet. When students try to find letters in the alphabet, observe whether they recognize letters immediately or if they return to the beginning to recite and point until they reach the targeted letter.

Integrate these alphabet lessons at the pacing that is most productive for students. Children who know very few letters will benefit from the activities *Starting With Children's Names* and *One Child's Name*. These activities personalize the alphabet and help children make connections between letters and the important people in their life.

Throughout the preschool and kindergarten years, alphabet books should be shared with students. Alphabet books are full of humor and imaginative artwork that fascinate and engage children as they teach both letter names and letter sounds. See *WTW* for a list of titles that we especially like.

Other activities in *Words Their Way* are also very suitable for the study of capital and lowercase letters. They include *One Child's Name, Alphabet Eggs* (on the *Words Their Way* CD-ROM), *Alphabet Concentration*, and *Letter Spin*. Sharing alphabet books is essential; we list some of our favorites in *Words Their Way*.

SORT 12   ALPHABET TRACKING STRIP

We have provided an alphabet tracking strip on page 60 that can be used in a variety of ways. You can use it as is, or cut it apart and glue it together to create one long strip. Make one for children to take home, to keep at their seats, or to use in small groups. Alphabet strips can be posted in the writing center and used as a reference during writing activities. While commercial alphabet charts may be posted for reference, young children will benefit more from having an alphabet strip within easy reach that they can touch and study up close.

Here are some things you can do with the strip:

1. Tracking practice: Provide all students with a strip and ask them to touch the letters as they recite or sing the alphabet song. Do this over and over to reinforce letter recognition, sequence, left-to-right orientation, and return sweep. You should periodically try saying the letters backwards by starting at Z.

2. Have children find and touch letters on their strip as you or another child calls them aloud. For example: "Find and touch the letter *p*. Find the letter at the beginning of Todd's name. Find the letter you need to spell the first sound in *turtle*." If you feature children's names as described in *Words Their Way* under *Starting With One Child's Name*, have children find all the letters in the name of the featured child.

3. You can use the alphabet strip as a record of the letters that students know by coloring in the letter boxes as they are mastered.

4. Give students a second strip and ask them to cut apart the letters. (Enlarge the strip to maximum size before making copies.) Then ask the students to put the letters back in order (with or without a second strip as a reference, depending on the student's skill level). These can be glued down.

5. Cut apart the alphabet strip to serve as the letter headers for the alphabet scrapbook described in *Words Their Way*.

SORT 13   FONT SORTS AND MATCHING CAPITAL AND LOWERCASE LETTERS

Students in the emergent stage who are learning their letters need to learn both uppercase and lowercase forms, and this can take some time.

Notes for the Teacher

While the capital and lowercase forms of some letters vary only in size (such as *S* and *s*), others look very different (such as *A* and *a*). Lowercase letters are sometimes called "little" letters, but lowercase *l* is really no smaller than capital *I*, so that term is somewhat ambiguous. We prefer to use the term "capital" for the uppercase letters and lowercase for the others. Young readers must also learn to recognize letters despite the variation in letter styles that abound in the world of print. Obvious examples include the lowercase *g* and *a* found in most printed material that look very different from the manuscript form teachers are likely to model in their writing or have on alphabet charts in the classroom. Less obvious, but still potentially confusing, are serifs, curly tails, and variations in line width. For this reason we feel it is helpful to draw students' attention to these differences and even to celebrate the rich variety through font sorts and font searches.

We have included a set of blackline masters on pages 61–69 that have five different font styles for each capital and lowercase letter. We suggest that you select from these as you study the letters both for letter recognition and letter sound connections. For example, if you are focusing upon the letters *B* and *M*, make a copy of the *B* and *M* font sorts and create a center activity or develop a handout for students to cut apart and sort for seatwork. Enlarge these as much as 50% for modeling or for use in centers. You may also want to paste them on squares of a heavier paper such as construction paper or cardstock and laminate them. Be sure to use the same color for all the cards, or a random assortment of colors so that color does not offer a clue for sorting.

Introducing the Sorts

When font sorts are first introduced they should be modeled by the teacher. Begin by laying out all the letter cards (both capital and lowercase) for one letter so that children can see them all. Use as a header the letter cards you think your students are most likely to recognize. (We used *Century Gothic* for the first column as it seems closest to the manuscript used in primary classrooms.) Explain, "Here is capital *A* and here is lowercase *a*." Select another letter card and think aloud as you explain. "Hmmm this looks a little different because it has fat lines (or curly lines, slants, etc.) but it is still a capital *A*, so I am going to put it under the other capital *A*." Continue like this for one or two more cards and then invite your students to choose a card, talk about it, and sort it under either the capital or the lowercase header. See if they can articulate some of the differences using their own terminology.

Sort, Check, and Reflect

Mix up all the letters except the headers and have the children sort them again under your supervision. Talk about how letters come in both capital and lowercase forms and how we use capitals for the first letter in names. Look around the classroom for more examples and ask students to find and point to specific letters in the charts they are using for shared reading.

Extend

On another day add a second set of letters so that you have two capital and two lowercase letters to compare. Start with obvious contrasts like *A* and *B*, but at some point try contrasting letters that children often confuse such as *B* and *D* or *P* and *Q*. When comparing the lowercase forms of those letters draw a line along the bottom of the letter cards so that students can orient them correctly. Eventually you can contrast up to four letters at a time.

Encourage children to go on letter hunts at home or at school, looking through newspapers, magazines, advertisements, and so on to find even more examples of letter styles. Children can add these to their own Alphabet Scrapbooks, described in Chapter 4 of *WTW*, or they can put them on a sheet of construction paper and post them in the classroom. Later these sheets can become pages and be made into a big book of letters. Pictures of things that begin with the letter's sound can also be added.

Read To: Literature Link

Martin, B., & Archambault, J. (1989). *Chicka chicka boom boom*. New York: Scholastic. *Chicka Chicka Boom Boom* is a favorite alphabet book because it features a cast of characters that includes the lowercase adventurous "kids" who must be comforted by the capital letter "mamas and papas, uncles and aunts" when they fall out of the coconut tree. See *Words Their Way* for ideas about using this as the basis for sorting boards and activities.

SORT 14   LETTER LOTTO

Students enjoy playing lotto with their letters. A 16-square blackline is included on page 70 as a template. Make boards by either writing letters in the squares or by pasting letters from the font sort in sort 13. Have students draw from a pile, call out the letter, and place a bingo marker on the matching letter. Later, students will play a similar game with beginning sounds; see *Initial Sound Bingo* in *WTW* among the activities with beginners in the letter name–alphabetic stage.

SORT 12   Alphabet Tracking Strip

Touch and name each letter.

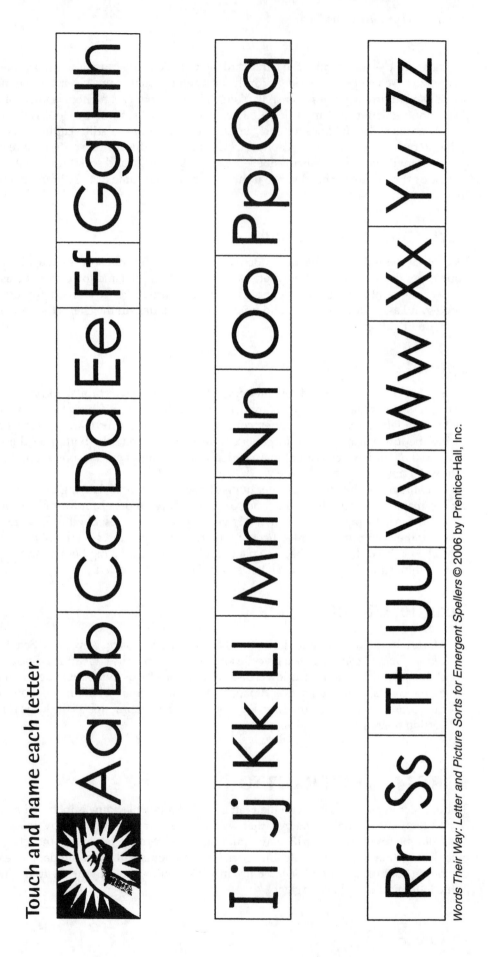

	Aa	Bb	Cc	Dd	Ee	Ff	Gg	Hh

Ii	Jj	Kk	Ll	Mm	Nn	Oo	Pp	Qq

Rr	Ss	Tt	Uu	Vv	Ww	Xx	Yy	Zz

SORT 13 Font Sorts and Matching Capital and Lowercase Letters

a	*a*	a	a	ə
A	*A*	A	A	A
b	*b*	b	b	b
B	*B*	B	B	B
C	*C*	C	C	C
C	*C*	C	C	C

d	*d*	d	**d**	d
D	***D***	D	**D**	D
e	***e***	e	**e**	e
E	***E***	E	**E**	E
f	***f***	f	**f**	f
F	***F***	F	**F**	F

g	*g*	g	**g**	g
G	*G*	G	**G**	G
h	*h*	h	**h**	h
H	*H*	H	**H**	H
i	*i*	i	**i**	i
I	*I*	I	**I**	I

Words Their Way: Letter and Picture Sorts for Emergent Spellers © 2006 by Prentice-Hall, Inc.

j	*j*	j	**J**	j
l	*J*	J	**J**	J
k	*k*	k	**k**	k
K	*K*	K	**K**	K
l	*l*	l	l	l
L	*L*	L	**L**	L

Words Their Way: Letter and Picture Sorts for Emergent Spellers © 2006 by Prentice-Hall, Inc.

m	*m*	m	**m**	m
M	*M*	M	**M**	M
n	*n*	n	**n**	n
N	*N*	N	**N**	N
o	*o*	o	**o**	o
O	*O*	O	**O**	O

p	*p*	p	**p**	p
P	*P*	P	**P**	P
q	*q*	q	**q**	q
Q	*Q*	Q	**Q**	Q
r	*r*	r	**r**	r
R	*R*	R	**R**	R

Words Their Way: Letter and Picture Sorts for Emergent Spellers © 2006 by Prentice-Hall, Inc.

S	*S*	S	**S**	ꕤ
S	*S*	S	**S**	ꕤ
t	*t*	t	**t**	t
T	*T*	T	**T**	T
U	*u*	U	**u**	U
U	*U*	U	**U**	U

Words Their Way: Letter and Picture Sorts for Emergent Spellers © 2006 by Prentice-Hall, Inc.

V	**V**	V	**V**	V
V	**V**	V	**V**	V
W	**W**	W	**W**	W
W	**W**	W	**W**	W
X	**X**	X	**X**	X
X	**X**	X	**X**	X

Words Their Way: Letter and Picture Sorts for Emergent Spellers © 2006 by Prentice-Hall, Inc.

y	y	y	y	y
Y	Y	Y	Y	y
Z	z	z	z	z
Z	Z	Z	Z	z

SORT 14 Letter Lotto Board

ACTIVITIES FOR

Concept of Word in Print

NOTES FOR THE TEACHER

This series of activities and sorts features the development of concept of word in print. Read With selections are followed by pictures to match to the sequence of events, as well as sentence strips and word cards to match. Repeated practice in tracking these familiar sentences helps students to acquire concept of word. Children who have a concept of word will also benefit from these activities as they begin to acquire sight words that are added to a cumulative word bank. Additional information about concept of word and activities are presented in Chapters 4 and 5 of *Words Their Way*.

The accompanying word study activities differ for students according to your assessment of students' phonological awareness, alphabet knowledge, and concept of word in print. Continue with alphabet and phonological awareness activities, especially with those students learning the alphabet. Students who know the letters of the alphabet are ready to spend more time studying the sounds of beginning consonants in sorts 15–27. These are the same students who begin to acquire sight words or words they can read from memory.

Late emergent spellers recognize all letters easily, and they build a sight vocabulary of perhaps 20 words. Kindergarten students may be required, and indeed do learn many sight words through extensive repeated practice. Memory of words is easier when children have a concept of word and know letter-sound correspondences. So these concept-of-word activities and studying beginning sounds thoroughly are important and should be done concurrently. Students in the next stage, letter name–alphabetic, have a solid concept of word and can consistently spell the beginning and ending sounds of words and so are in a much better position to retain words in memory.

STANDARD ROUTINES

1. Read With

As described earlier, there are three basic steps in a concept of word activity for emergent learners:

- Enlarge the text so that everyone in the group can easily see it. This can be done by creating an overhead, by printing the selection on a chart, or by creating sentence strips for a pocket chart. Read the text repeatedly together so that children memorize the text. The teacher should model fingerpointing.
- Invite children to individually point to the words and make individual copies of the selection so that every child can fingerpoint. Individual copies can be placed in personal readers.

• Locate words or letters in the text and collect known words as sight words into a word bank.

With groups of early emergent spellers, students fingerpoint read one or two lines, and students in the later part of this stage read 2–4 lines of text. Note how accurately students fingerpoint read as they reread the familiar selections. Here are the titles of the Read With selections presented thus far that you can add to the other selections you read with your students in this part.

Sort 1 *My Fruit*   Sort 2 *Circles*
Sort 3 *Animals*   Sort 4 *Socks, Shoes, Caps, and Gloves*
Sort 6 *Oh, A-Hunting We Will Go*   Sort 7 *Open and Close*

2. Sentence Strips and Cut-Up Sentences

Some of the selections come with sentence strips that can be cut apart and then matched back to the text. To demonstrate how to match, begin with a sentence from a familiar text and write it on a sentence strip. Show students how you match the strip back to the text. Reread the words to see if the sentence sounds the same. Sentence strips can also be cut into words. Students are then asked to rebuild the sentence by matching words back to a copy of the sentence or by memory. Students will need to consider at least the beginning sounds to get words in the right order.

3. Find Words / Letters You Know

Call out two or three words or letters for all students to find either on the enlarged copy of the selection or on their own copies. They can simply point to the words and letters or they can underline or highlight them on their individual copies. With early emergent spellers, choose words or letters at the beginning or end of lines from their Read With materials. Students can also work in pairs and call out words and letters for their partners to find.

Demonstrate how to underline familiar words in text: "*I am going to point to words I know, words that I can read quickly, in a flash! If you read a word easily by itself, then use your pencil to underline the word.*" Show students how you make a line underneath a word. Some students like to circle their choices though this is messy. Print out an extra copy for such underlining. Pieces of Wicki Sticks, translucent highlighting tape, or post-its can be used to underline words on enlarged copies. If you use a pocket chart you might want to use rectangles cut from colored plastic overheads to highlight words. Just tuck the plastic in the pocket over the word. To see how well these words are known in isolation, ask students to read the underlined words that you point to in random order.

4. Collect Word and Letter Cards for Word Banks

Students who already have a concept of word and who are in the later part of this stage can collect one or two sight words from a selection that they have reread several times to add to a word bank. (Consult *Words Their Way* for more information about developing and using word banks.) After students find words they know, and you have asked them to read the words, write the words on word cards. Use index cards, tagboard, or card stock to cut a supply of cards. One-inch by 3-inch cards are a good size. At the emergent stage there will not be many words to keep track of. They can be stored in plastic bags or on a ring. Students who do not have a concept of word in print may not be able to collect sight words, so we can use this as an opportunity to ask them to identify letters. Have students point to letters they know as you write them on cards.

5. Record Words and Letters I Read

Record students' known words or letters on either the *Words I Read* or *Letters I Read* form on pages 81 and 82 and keep this form in their personal readers. There is a place to log the date of the entries. To make it easier to return to context, number the selections in students' personal readers and record the story number. Directions to organize personal readers are presented in Chapter 5 of *Words Their Way*.

6. Word Hunts

After collecting some words or letters, students take turns showing other students what they have. Students ask each other, "*Does anyone have the word/letter _____?*" Students find their matches, hold them up, say the word or letter, and return them to their word or letter piles.

7. Word Study for Beginning Consonants

The reading selections that follow can be used as a starting point or follow-up for word study activities that focus on initial consonant sounds. For example, the first selection, *Rain on the Green Grass*, is a natural link with the initial sound for *r*. After reading the selections students can be asked to find words that start with *r* and, with the pictures from the letter pages in sorts 15 through 27, pages 129–147, students are then provided with pictures of things that start with *r* to contrast with other sounds they have studied. Or, after studying the sound of *r*, they can revisit the familiar selection to hunt for words. The study of beginning consonants is described in more detail in the next unit, but we will make suggestions throughout this unit about consonant study that you might follow in connection with these selections.

EASY READ WITH SELECTIONS

SELECTION 1: RAIN ON THE GREEN GRASS AND ASSESSMENT

All along, you have observed if students can point accurately to the words as they recite the familiar materials in the selections. With this selection we offer a point scale to assess concept of word.

Based on the PALS assessment, *Rain on the Green Grass* is a selection with benchmarks for students at the end of preschool or early in kindergarten. Introduce children to *Rain on the Green Grass*, on page 83, reading it several times while you model pointing. Give each student a copy to practice pointing. Then assess children individually by asking them to read the memorized rhyme as you use the scale described below. At the end of this supplement, the Humpty Dumpty rhyme is presented with benchmark scores for students eight or nine months into kindergarten.

The end of prekindergarten range score is 8–15 points as reported in the scoring guide from the Pre-K PALS, Fall 2001 (Invernizzi, Sullivan, & Meier, 2001).

Use this guide to score each line:
0 points – no attention to print
1 point – directionality with no clear pattern
2 points – points to letters
3 points – points rhythmically with stressed beats or syllables
4 points – points to some words, but gets off track
5 points – self-corrects when off track
6 points – points correctly

Rain on the Green Grass

Rain on the green grass, _____
and rain on the tree, _____
Rain on the rooftop, _____
But not on me! _____

End of Pre-K Benchmark Range: 8–15   Score: _____/24

Word Study for Sounds

Ask students to find the words that rhyme. Ask students for words that start with *r* (*rain*), *b* (*but*), *n* (*not*), or *m* (*me*). Sort pictures that begin with these sounds as a follow-up to the concept of word activities.

Read To: Literature Links

Arnosky, J. (1997). *Rabbits and raindrops*. New York: Putnam.
Hesse, K., & Muth, J. J. (1999). *Come on, rain!* New York: Scholastic.
Hoban, J. (1989). *Amy loves the rain*. New York: HarperCollins.
Yashimo, T. (1958). *Umbrella*. New York: Viking.

SELECTION 2: PEAS PORRIDGE HOT

Explain to students that porridge is like oatmeal (see page 84). The second stanza ("*Some like it hot . . .* ") is quite easy and a favorite of students just acquiring concept of word in print. Students use the word cards on the blackline on page 85 to match underneath the first line of the rhyme.

Peas Porridge Hot

Peas porridge hot,
Peas porridge cold,
Peas porridge in the pot
Nine days old.

Some like it hot,
Some like it cold,
Some like it in the pot
Nine days old!

Extend

Write the second stanza on a pocket chart or as a writing frame with blanks and have students substitute cards for key words:

> Substitute names for **Some**: *Rodney likes it hot . . .*
> Substitute temperatures for **hot**: *Some like it freezing . . .*
> Substitute numbers for **Nine**: *Seven days old.*

Word Study for Sounds

Ask students to find the words that rhyme. Ask students for words that start with *p* (*peas, porridge, pot*), *h* (*hot*), *l* (*like*), and *n* (*nine*). Sort pictures that begin with these sounds as a follow-up to the concept of word activities.

Dramatization

Students enjoy changing their faces as they attempt to taste the porridge *hot, cold,* and a yucky *nine days old*! Practice stirring the porridge and tasting it in small groups.

SELECTION 3: JUMP ROPE, JUMP ROPE

Students chant as they pretend to jump rope and will enjoy the chant on the playground as they jump rope. Point out the question mark and exclamation mark on page 86 and model how to interpret the punctuation. Show students how the voice rises at the question mark and the final line is read with excitement.

> *Jump Rope, Jump Rope*
>
> Jump rope, jump rope,
> Will I miss?
>
> Jump rope, jump rope,
> Just watch this!

Word Study for Sounds

Ask students to find the words that rhyme. Ask students to think of words that start with *j* (*jump, just*), *r* (*rope*), *w* (*will, watch*), and *m* (*miss*). Sort pictures that begin with these sounds as a follow-up to the concept of word activities.

SELECTION 4: MY FAMILY SITS ON THE BED

This cumulative story on page 87 has pictures to match to the side of each line. Students use the word cards on the blackline on page 88 to match underneath the first line of the rhyme. There are more two- and three-syllable words in this selection than in previous selections, so students may need some guidance as they attempt to point. Model how we touch words for each syllable.

My Family Sits on the Bed
My mama sits on the bed.

My papa sits on the bed.

My sister sits on the bed.

My dog sits on the bed.

Extend

In a small group, use frame sentences in a pocket chart to substitute words that come to mind. Ask students to tell you an animal that sits on the bed whose name begins with the /c/ sound: "*My cat sits on the bed.*" Students can call out their own substitutions: "*My grand-mother sits on the bed.*" Other words can be substituted for *sits*: "*My sister jumps on the bed.*"

Students can make up their own verses that can be typed in 26-point text and placed in students' personal readers. For example, students can use different verbs instead of *sits*: "*My mama sings with me. My papa dances with me. My sister runs with me.*" Students like to act out and then read about animals and their movements: "*My monkey climbs on the bed. My monkey jumps on the bed.*"

Read To: Literature Links

Christalow, E. (1999). *Five little monkeys jumping on the bed.* Boston: Clarion.
Peek, M. (1981). *Roll over: A country song.* Boston: Houghton.
Wood, A. (1984). *The napping house.* New York: Harcourt.

Word Study for Sounds

Ask students for words that start with *m* (*my*), *f* (*family*), *b* (*bed*), *s* (*sits, sister*), and so on. Sort pictures that begin with these sounds as a follow-up to the concept of word activities.

English Language Learners

English language learners may read a translation with ease. For example,

> *Mi familia se sienta en la cama*
>
> Mi mama se sienta en la cama.
> Mi papa se sienta en la cama.
> Mi hermana se sienta en la cama.
> Mi perro se sienta en la cama.

SELECTION 5: ROW, ROW, ROW YOUR BOAT

"Row, Row, Row Your Boat" is a well-known song, so begin singing it. Then point out the words, using a copy of page 89. The single-syllable words in the first line make this selection easy for early emergent readers to track. Observe how students fingerpoint read *Gently* in the second line. *Merrily* on the third line is even more difficult to track. To find their way, students should use their knowledge of the letter *m* to track from one *merrily* to the next.

> *Row, Row, Row Your Boat*
>
> Row, row, row your boat
> Gently down the stream.
> Merrily, merrily, merrily,
> Life is but a dream.

Word Study for Sounds

Ask students to find the words that rhyme. Ask students for words that start with *r* (*row*), *b* (*boat, but*), *l* (*life*), *m* (*merrily*), and so on. Sort pictures that begin with these sounds as a follow-up to the concept of word activities.

Extend

Substitute different movements for different forms of transportation:

> Dance, dance, dance your feet,
> Run, run, run your feet,
> Ride, ride, ride your bike,
> Drive, drive, drive your car,
> All the way to the movies / baseball game / school / Sarah's house.

SELECTION 6: ONE, TWO, BUCKLE MY SHOE

The numbers and rhythm of this rhyme, shown on page 90, make it a fun one to track. You will see a child on the *Words Their Way* Video attempting to point to the words in this rhyme who is almost in control of her fingerpointing. Two weeks after we recorded her pointing to *buckle* while saying *"buckle my"* she was able to point correctly. Students can be asked to hold up the correct number of fingers as they recite the rhyme. Students can also sort the pictures to the right of each line and use the word cards on the black-line on page 91 to match underneath the first line of this rhyme.

One, Two, Buckle My Shoe

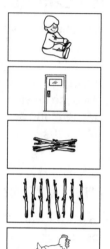

One, two, buckle my shoe,

Three, four, shut the door.

Five, six, pick up sticks.

Seven, eight lay them straight.

Nine, ten, a big fat hen.

As they refer to the rhyme, have students place the numbers in order.

Word Study for Sounds

Ask students to find the words that rhyme.

Ask students for words that start with *t* (*two, ten*), *b* (*buckle, big*), *f* (*four, five, fat*), *h* (*hen*), and so on. Sort pictures from the sorts that follow that begin with these sounds as a follow-up to the concept of word activities.

Extend

Show students how to play "pick up sticks" as they learn this rhyme. They can be asked to pick up the number you call out: *"Pick up two sticks, now four, . . ."* and so on.

SELECTION 7: HAPPY BIRTHDAY

The familiar song on page 92 is celebratory and can be used whenever a child has a birthday. The two-syllable words offer a challenge in pointing for early emergent readers. Sing *Happy Birthday* and track the song on a chart. Make a word card of the student's name to attach to the end of the third line. When it is a student's birthday, give the student a special copy of this page with his or her name written in special writing in a bold color or gold marker. A pocket chart makes it easy to add students' names.

Happy Birthday

Happy Birthday to you,
Happy Birthday to you,
Happy Birthday dear _____,
Happy Birthday to you.

Word Study for Sounds

Ask students for words that start with *h* (*happy*), *b* (*birthday*), *d* (*dear*), *t* (*to*), or *y* (*you*). Sort pictures that begin with these sounds as a follow-up to the concept of word activities.

Read To: Literature Links

There are many picture books that celebrate birthdays. Here are a few.

Hill, E. (1981). *Spot's birthday*. New York: Putnam.
Hutchins, P. (1978). *Happy birthday Sam*. New York: Greenwillow.
Keats, E. J. (1968). *A letter to Amy*. New York: HarperCollins.
Peek, M. (1985). *Mary wore her red dress and Henry wore his green sneakers*. Boston: Clarion.
Rice, E. (1981). *Benny bakes a cake*. New York: Greenwillow.

Sound Play

Some students like to play a sound game in which they substitute a different sound at the beginning of the words: "*Pappy Pirthday, Dappy Dirthday,*" and so on. See Yopp, H. K. (1992). Developing phonemic awareness in young children. *The Reading Teacher*, 45.

Extend

Blow out the candle. Students enjoy pretending to blow out candles. If students are studying letters and sounds, you can change the blowing to a whispered beginning consonant: "*Let's blow with the beginning sounds we have been studying. Who has a letter or sound in mind?*" Use *m* or *mmmm*. "*Okay, let's pretend we are blowing out the candles. Mmmm. That doesn't work; my lips are together. Who has another letter?*" *Pppppp* and *tttt* are ejective or plosive sounds to consider next. Students enjoy finding the sounds that offer the greatest "puff" of air.

SELECTION 8 *HUMPTY DUMPTY* AND CONCEPT OF WORD IN PRINT REVIEW

The nursery rhyme on page 93 is a favorite. At the end of this supplement, we return to this rhyme to assess concept of word in print. The first two lines are particularly good to assess whether students can handle two-syllable words as they point. If students are repeatedly unable to point accurately as they read the two-syllable words, continue to practice rereading materials that are composed mostly of single-syllable words.

Word Study for Sounds

Ask students to find the words that rhyme. Ask students for words that start with *h* (*Humpty, had, horses*), *w* (*wall*), *k* (*king*), *f* (*fall*), or *m* (*men*). Sort pictures that begin with these sounds as a follow-up to the concept of word activities.

Picture Match for *Humpty Dumpty*

From their copies of the blackline on page 94, have students cut the pictures and sequence them in the order of the events in *Humpty Dumpty*. Show them that the pictures can also match lines in the nursery rhyme. Students can paste these pictures either in order at the top of the rhyme or they can paste each picture beside its corresponding line.

Underlined words are identified by students in the concept of word assessment in the next section to assess emergent literacy, page 148.

Humpty Dumpty

<u>Humpty</u> Dumpty sat on a <u>wall</u>.
Humpty <u>Dumpty</u> had a great <u>fall</u>.
<u>All</u> the <u>king's</u> horses
<u>And</u> all the king's <u>men</u>
Couldn't <u>put</u> Humpty <u>together</u> again!

Read To: Literature Links in Spanish

Here is a good source of easy songs in Spanish:

Orozco, J-L. (1996). *De colores and other Latin-American folk songs for children*. New York: Dutton Children's Books.
Lyrics are in Spanish and English, with arrangements. *La araña peqieñita* (*Eensy Weensy Spider*) and the counting song, *Les Elefantes* (*The Elephant Song*), are included. You'll find Spanish sounds that are similar to English sounds.

Collect a variety of nursery rhyme books and look up this rhyme to compare how different artists have illustrated it. Compare the words to see if they are the same.

Words I Read

		Reads		
Date	Story Number		Date	Story Number

Words _____

Letters I Read

Letters		Reads	
A a		N n	
B b		O o	
C c		P p	
D d		Q q	
E e		R r	
F f		S s	
G g		T t	
H h		U u	
I i		V v	
J j		W w	
K k		X x	
L l		Y y	
M m		Z z	

Words Their Way: Letter and Picture Sorts for Emergent Spellers © 2006 by Prentice-Hall, Inc.

Name_____   Date/Story Number_____

Rain on the Green Grass

Rain on the green grass,

and rain on the tree,

Rain on the housetop,

But not on me.

Words Their Way: Letter and Picture Sorts for Emergent Spellers © 2006 by Prentice-Hall, Inc.

Name_____   Date/Story Number_____

Peas Porridge Hot

Peas porridge hot,

Peas porridge cold,

Peas porridge in the pot

Nine days old.

Some like it hot,

Some like it cold,

Some like it in the pot

Nine days old!

Some like it hot			
Some	like	it	hot
cold	nine	one	two
three	four	five	six
seven	eight	1	2
3	4	5	6
7	8	9	

Words Their Way: Letter and Picture Sorts for Emergent Spellers © 2006 by Prentice-Hall, Inc.

Name_____   Date/Story Number_____

Jump Rope, Jump Rope

Jump rope, jump rope,

Will I miss?

Jump rope, jump rope,

Just watch this!

Name_____   Date/Story Number_____

My Family Sits on the Bed

My mama sits on the bed.

My papa sits on the bed.

My sister sits on the bed.

My dog sits on the bed.

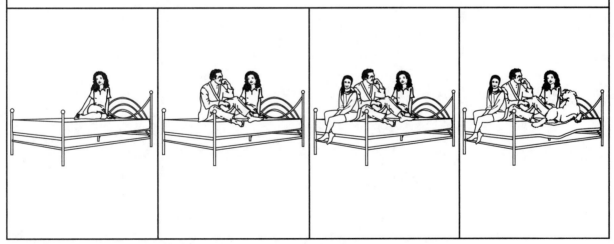

Words Their Way: Letter and Picture Sorts for Emergent Spellers © 2006 by Prentice-Hall, Inc.

My mama sits on the bed.		
My	mama	sits
on	the	bed.
papa	sister	dog

Words Their Way: Letter and Picture Sorts for Emergent Spellers © 2006 by Prentice-Hall, Inc.

Name _____   Date/Story Number_____

Row, Row, Row Your Boat

Row, row, row your boat

Gently down the stream.

Merrily, merrily, merrily,

Life is but a dream.

Words Their Way: Letter and Picture Sorts for Emergent Spellers © 2006 by Prentice-Hall, Inc.

Name_____   Date/Story Number_____

One, Two, Buckle My Shoe

One, two, buckle my shoe,

Three, four, shut the door.

Five, six, pick up sticks.

Seven, eight lay them straight.

Nine, ten, a big fat hen.

One, two, buckle my shoe.		
One	two	buckle
my	shoe.	

Three, four, shut the door.		
Three	four	shut
the	door.	

Words Their Way: Letter and Picture Sorts for Emergent Spellers © 2006 by Prentice-Hall, Inc.

Name_____   Date/Story Number_____

Happy Birthday

Happy Birthday to you,

Happy Birthday to you,

Happy Birthday dear _____,

Happy Birthday to you.

Name_____ Date/Story Number_____

Humpty Dumpty

Humpty Dumpty sat on a wall.

Humpty Dumpty had a great fall.

All the king's horses

And all the king's men

Couldn't put Humpty together again!

Words Their Way: Letter and Picture Sorts for Emergent Spellers © 2006 by Prentice-Hall, Inc.

Humpty Dumpty sat on a wall.		
Humpty	Dumpty	sat
on	a	wall.

Humpty Dumpty had a great fall.		
Humpty	Dumpty	had
a	great	fall.

SORTS 15–27

Teaching Beginning Consonant Sounds

NOTES FOR THE TEACHER

In this unit we provide you with resources for the teaching of beginning consonant sounds. For each beginning sound there is a *letter page* that has pictures for sorting beginning with *s*. Children cannot sort unless they have two or more sounds to contrast, but we have created these one-sound pages to make it easier to sequence and group sounds to match any core reading program.

In the sequence presented here, beginning consonant sounds are divided into groups of four. Two letters are presented in each of the first two sorts, and then the four letters are combined for sorting, review, and assessment. This sequence reflects one way to organize beginning consonant sound study.

Additional pictures for many of the sounds can be found in *Words Their Way*. By clipping the pictures and arranging them on a template supplied in *Words Their Way* (p. 405), it is easy to create handouts that children cut apart and sort. The letter lotto board on page 70 can be used as a template. On these templates you can mix two or more sounds, as you will see in the examples in *Words Their Way*. In this way you can control the sequence. The *Words Their Way* CD-ROM has prepared sets of initial sounds sorts that contrast three sounds at a time as well as prepared game boards. *Words Their Way: Word Sorts for Letter Name–Alphabetic Spellers*, the next book in this series, has prepared sorts that contrast four sounds. This variety of resources enables you to take many different paths for the study of initial sounds depending on your students' needs and the sequence preferred.

All students in the emergent stage should participate in these activities, but some students will be able to handle a faster pace with more categories. If students are struggling to sort accurately, spend a bit more time on two sounds, and then add a third and a fourth. To sustain interest, choose letters or sounds that have personal relevance. If the student's name is Pat, for example, a one-sentence dictation, like "*Pat* is my name," is reread several times a day, and the student might be given words that begin with *p* and *t* for sorting.

Across the emergent stage, developmental level determines pacing:

- Early emergent spellers learn how we listen for sounds at the beginning of words. They learn the names of frequent letters and they learn basic strokes in handwriting.
- Middle level emergent learners may begin these activities with some awareness of letter-sound correspondences. They practice making the letters, learn the names of the letters, and sort pictures that offer a clear contrast (such as *m* and *s*) into two or more categories at a time.

- Late emergent spellers know most letters of the alphabet and may know some letter-sound correspondences. They will benefit from repeated practice that increases the accuracy and speed of their sorting. They can sort less obvious contrasts (like *b* and *p*) and learn the less frequent sounds (like *y* and *w*). Late emergent spellers in first grade may benefit from a fast-paced review of initial consonants that contrast up to four sounds at a time as supplied in the first section of the *Words Their Way: Word Sorts for Letter Name–Alphabetic Spellers* companion book.

At the emergent level it is particularly important to introduce sounds and letters in meaningful contexts so that students can see the purpose for learning those confusing little black marks and those abstract sounds. For this reason we provide reading selections to use as a starting point for the study of letter-sound correspondences and we refer you back to earlier selections, particularly in the concept of word activities. We encourage you to look through your own collections of favorite poems, jingles, chart stories, big books, and so on for texts that feature particular letters. *Mrs. Wishy Washy*, a favorite book from the Wright Group Story Box (by Joy Cowley), is a natural link with the letter *w*. *Jump Frog, Jump* (by Robert Kalen) features the word *jump* throughout and therefore links to the letter *j*. Themes and topics of study can also become the starting point for word study. For example, in February ask students to dictate sentences about valentines and then introduce or review the sound of the letter *v*.

Chapter 4 of *Words Their Way* provides additional background information about consonants and guidelines for sorting. You will find games in the activities section of that chapter, such as Letter Spin and Follow the Path, that extend children's learning as they continue to practice in engaging ways.

Sounds Across Languages: Word Study with English Language Learners

Many of the pictures that students use first in concept sorts are repeated in the beginning sound pictures, and this will support English language learners. Children love to work in pairs, and this is especially helpful for English language learners. The English-speaking child can name the pictures that an English language learner child might not know. When students do not know the name of several pictures in a sort, have them focus on the pictures that they do know, and, if possible, find words and pictures that begin in the student's oral language. A translation dictionary can provide words to consider in students' heritage languages. We can also ask students, "*What words can you think of in _____, the language you speak at home, that sound like this word, _____, at the beginning?*"

For each group of consonants in Sorts 15–27, some of the sound properties of these letters and the associations that students make are discussed to provide a sense of the types of confusions or substitutions that are common. For example, students with Spanish-language backgrounds may respond that *house* and *José* sound alike at the beginning.

The sequence of word study instruction for students from a Spanish-language background should be based on what they know about letter-sound correspondences, just as it is for English-speaking children. The Spanish Elementary Spelling Inventory in *Words Their Way*, developed by Lori Helman, and the sorts on the *Words Their Way* CD-ROM show what students know about letter-sound correspondences in Spanish. Students may know a good deal more about the Spanish vowels than students at the same stage know about English vowels because there are fewer vowel sounds in Spanish and the sounds are more uniform in pronunciation.

There are five sorts on the *Words Their Way* CD-ROM that contrast consonants using Spanish words to match the pictures (*s m p, l c v, j d f, g r y, z ch ll*). What children know in Spanish transfers to their learning in English. Late in the *emergente* stage (emergent stage in Spanish) students write S or U for *suma*, and in the early *nombre de letra alfabética* stage (the letter name–alphabetic stage in English) students study the syllables *ma, me, mi, mo,* and *mu* (*mano, meta, mira, moto, mudo*).

Teaching Consonant Blends and Digraphs, Final Consonant Sounds, and Vowels

Consonant blends and digraphs are generally studied in the letter name–alphabetic stage as described in Chapter 5 of *Words Their Way*. Right after students master beginning consonants, they study digraphs and learn that consonant digraphs make one new sound, not just a combination of two letters. The letter *q* is not presented here as it is studied as a blend, /kw/.

Emergent learners in English do not use vowels often in their writing unless they are letter names, as in the long vowels. They hear the most salient consonant sounds, and this is why students study the letter-sound correspondences for consonant sounds first in developmentally based word study. Vowel sounds are first studied in the next supplement in this series, *Words Their Way: Word Sorts for Letter Name–Alphabetic Spellers*, when students examine the rime as seen in word families; for example, /-at/, /-ed/. When students begin to use vowels in their spelling they have the phonemic awareness to attend to them and are ready to study them.

You may study some final sounds once students have a firm understanding of several beginning consonant sounds. For example, you may extend the pronunciation of the final sound at the end of *bat* (*batah*) and observe how students recognize the final sounds of similar words. "Do *bat* and *car* sound alike at the end? Do *hat* and *goat* sound alike at the end?" Many students' oral language backgrounds and dialects do not include the same final sounds, and there will be deletions in spelling that are common to particular dialects in your area. Across several languages, we have found confusions around these final sounds: /-s/, /-t/, /-d/, /-p/, /-l/, /-r/, /-z/.

All these features are also introduced to some extent as we write with children in activities such as Morning Message or when we take dictations. We model how we segment all the phonemes (including blends, digraphs, and vowels) and match them to letters. When students write encourage them to listen for other sounds in the words and represent them as best they can. By modeling and encouraging you can foreshadow the formal study of blends, digraphs, and vowels in the letter name–alphabetic stage.

INTRODUCING THE BEGINNING CONSONANT PICTURE SORTS

Continue to use the four basic steps in a small group word study activity: Demonstrate, Sort and Check, Reflect, and Extend. These directions will give you some idea of how to use the letter pages.

Demonstrate the Sort

Introduce the key pictures at the bottom of the letter pages as in this example using the M sheet. Pointing to the key picture, you might say, "Do you know what this is? Yes, *mouse*. And here you can see the beginning letter in *mouse*; it is an *m*. Say *mouse* for me. *Mouse*." To draw the sound out, say the beginning consonant sound slowly: "Listen to the sound at the beginning of mouse, *Mmmmouse*." Have students repeat this with you.

You can also isolate the sound and then say the word (/m/ *mouse*). Read and name the other pictures together. If you are introducing another new sound at the time, such as *s*, repeat with the other letter.

Introduce the sort by placing the key letters and pictures (*mouse* and *sun*) at the top of columns you will create on a tabletop, in a pocket chart, on an overhead, and so on. Discuss the letter cards that correspond to each column: "Here is the card with the capital and lowercase letters. Where should we put the *m*, with the picture of the mouse or the picture of the sun?" Be explicit as you explain why you sort the way you do. Now turn to the pictures on the letter page. "Here is a picture of a moon. *Moon* starts with the /m/ sound made by the letter *m*, so I will put it under the picture of the mouse. *Moon* and *mouse* begin with the same sound. This is a picture of socks. *Ssssocks* starts with the /s/ sound made by the letter *s*, so I will put the picture of socks under the picture of the sun." Model a few more matches in the same manner and then say, "*Now, please help me sort the rest of these pictures.*" Continue with the students' help to sort all of the pictures. When all the pictures have been sorted, name them in columns and check for any pictures that need to be changed: "*Do all of these sound alike at the beginning? Do we need to move any?*" This is the time to correct any errors students may have made.

Sort and Check

The second time students sort they should work more independently. You may sort as a group or you may give out sets of pictures to cut apart (or you may already have sets cut up to save time). Students can work in a small group, in pairs, or independently to sort by the key picture. Remind students to say the names of the pictures and key letters and pictures as they make matches. Show students how to check their columns by naming each picture and how to move pictures that do not belong.

Reflect

Involve students in a discussion of the sort: "*Why did we sort the way we did?*" Ask two or three students to explain their sorts.

Extend

It is important that students sort again over several days. If you use a pocket chart, make it available for sorting during the day. Students love to be the teacher and teach their classmates in just the same way you did. Students can sort their pictures again at their seats, in centers, or even at home. The weekly routines below describe more ways to extend the study of beginning consonants.

WEEKLY ROUTINES FOR BEGINNING CONSONANT SORTS 15-27

Continue to integrate word study into your literacy instruction through the essential literacy activities discussed earlier: Read To, Read With, Word Study, and Talk With. The group sorting lesson should be followed up with repeated sorts as well as the other activities described below so that students have ample practice. Students should be able to sort accurately and quickly. As they become more proficient at these activities they complete them independently. These and similar activities are discussed in Chapter 4 of *Words Their Way*.

Read To: Literature Links

Begin with literature in which sounds are embedded in rich oral language. Two types of literature are presented:

- Picture books that explore these beginning sounds are listed here. Other materials are listed in *Words Their Way*, Chapter 4. Alphabet books continue to be useful resources. If you are studying the letter *m*, have students find the pages in various books that feature the letter and show the group what they found—even preschoolers can use reference books!
- Selections of rhymes or brief stories are presented at the end of each series of sounds. They are fun to recite and sing, they support the development of concept of word in print, and they are used in word study activities.

Letter Page Activities

Beginning consonant picture sorts are provided on pages 129 to 147. Prepare for the sort by enlarging and cutting a demonstration set and by making a copy of the letter pages for each student in the group. There are three areas on each letter page.

1. Each page includes a collection of pictures for one beginning sound. These pictures are combined with another letter page for a contrast. The first card on the first row is the letter in both capital and lowercase. The second card is the underlined key picture to use as a header for the sort.

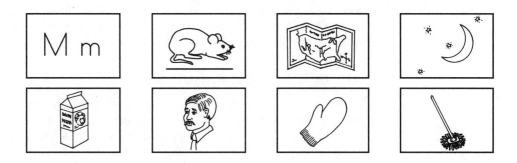

2. On the last two boxes of the third row, there is space for students to practice writing the letters. Point to the capital and lowercase letters saying, "Here are the capital and lowercase letters (*Mm*). Let me show you how to follow the arrows." Demonstrate at the table with students or on an overhead. Have students complete the letters on their own pages.

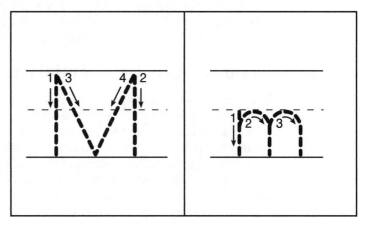

3. At the bottom of the page is a strip to introduce the sound. These strips are posted in Alphabet Scrapbooks or stapled together with other letter page strips. To the right of the picture is the letter in outline form followed by a line for Word Writing.

Some students may simply trace in the letter. The other students should be encouraged to write down "letters for all of the sounds you hear and feel when you say the name of this picture. You can hear and feel the beginning sound, the *mmmm* sound. Are there other sounds and letters that you hear or feel when you say *mouse*?" The final /s/ sound might be apparent to students. Show them how you write the *s* on the line.

Repeated Sorting

The primary activity students need to do across several days is to sort their pictures again. After cutting up the pictures they can be stored in baggies or envelopes labeled with the child's name to sort again. Some teachers create sets of pictures that they use from year to year that are colored and laminated for students to use in centers or small groups. Other teachers create sorting folders such as the ones described in *Words Their Way* for students to use. Chapter 3 of *Words Their Way* describes different options.

No-Peeking Buddy Sorts

No-peeking sorts were developed to use with words. Pictures do not offer clues to the spelling categories the way that words do. However, students can still work together in the same manner. Letters or key pictures are used as headers. One student names the picture drawn from a pile while the other students indicate under which picture the named picture goes.

Alphabet Scrapbooks

The Alphabet Scrapbooks described in the activities section of Chapter 4 in *Words Their Way* are a beginning dictionary that children create for themselves as they study letters and sounds. You may also want to compile a big book version using tag board or chart paper. This may begin as a bulletin board activity. In individual scrapbooks, students can paste the bottom strip of the letter page as the heading of each letter page.

Draw and Label/Cut and Paste

Students should be asked to think beyond the pictures given to them in the sort when they draw pictures or look for pictures of things that begin with a sound. These pictures may be added to Alphabet Scrapbooks, a class bulletin board, or a class big book. Oral brainstorming is helpful before students are asked to draw things as they may have difficulty thinking of words. You might also suggest that they use an alphabet book as a reference for ideas. English Language Learners may have difficulty thinking of English words. Be ready to accept words in their native language that they draw for you.

One way to manage "cut and paste" and make it into a group activity is with **Sound Buckets.** Introduce a small bucket or box for each sound and label it with the beginning letter and key picture. Have children find pictures, cut them out, and put them in the appropriate bucket. After a few days of collecting, students can join you in pasting them on a sheet of paper that can be posted on a bulletin board or made into the big class Alphabet Scrapbook.

Alphabet Sorts and Fonts

As you work through the different letters in these sorts, remember to add the appropriate font sorts as well from the Alphabet Unit. Children can look for capital and lowercase letters in newspapers and magazines and add them to Alphabet Scrapbooks.

Read With: Concept of Word in Print

The materials for Read With activities include rhymes, stories, and songs that children first learn to recite together as well as materials that students dictate. New selections are included here, and we suggest other materials to be typed and placed in students' personal readers for rereading. Choose one selection that is three or four lines long, type it in 26-point font, and make three copies: one for the personal reader, one to mark for known sight words, and another to take home. Students draw pictures to accompany these selections. Use these selections in the manner described in sort 15.

Word Hunts

After studying sets of sounds direct children's attention to familiar reading selections as well as other familiar literature for a word hunt. Challenge them to find words that begin with the sounds that they have been studying. Expect some confusions to arise, however. Accept words with blends, as when a child says that *grass* begins with *g*. When a child finds words with digraphs (as in the *s* of *shoe*) or with soft *g* (as in *gingerbread*), be ready to explain that some words begin with the same letter but have a different sound. You may want to record the words students find on a chart or in a class book of sounds. Students can underline or highlight words on their own copies of a selection, and may even write them in their own Alphabet Scrapbooks. Children should also check alphabet books and their word banks for words that begin with the sound of interest.

The Sound Board for Beginning Consonants and Digraphs in the Appendix of *Words Their Way* is a valuable tool to study beginning sounds. Each consonant sound is presented in this order: the capital and lowercase letters, a picture of a word that begins with that sound, and the written word for the picture (e.g. *Ss*, a picture of a sun, and the word *sun*). Students should have a copy of a sound board in their personal readers and writing books.

SORTS 15–17   BEGINNING CONSONANT SOUND SORTS FOR /S/, /M/, /B/, /R/

Notes for the Teacher

We recommend S, M, B, and R to begin the study of consonants. These first four sounds and letters are distinct both visually and in terms of their articulation, which makes it easier to contrast the sounds and letters. There are also many words that begin with these letters. Take time for repeated practice of these first four beginning consonant sounds, and later ones will come more easily.

Sounds Across Dialects and Languages

Many students cannot pronounce the /r/ sound easily, and confuse it with the /l/ sound. Some students may substitute the /s/ sound for the /sh/ sound. When students think of words that sound the same as other words, they may include words that sound the same in their dialect or language, but not yours. For example, a student may say *sew* for *show* and consider it to be an example of an *s* word. Accept students' contributions as accurate given their dialect. Pointing out the difference at that time may be useful, and these contrasts are made later when students have mastery of the basic contrasts. For example, after examining /b/ and /p/ separately, sorts 19 and 22 enable you to observe how students contrast these similar sounds. Spanish pronunciation may cause some confusion between /b/ and /v/. Students may say *very* as *berry*. The /r/ sound at the beginning may sound rolled as it would be in Spanish.

SORT 15 /S/, /M/ (pages 129 and 130)
SORT 16 /B/, /R/ (pages 131 and 132)
SORT 17 /S/, /M/, /B/, /R/ (pages 129–132)
Read To: Literature Links

Berenstein, S. & J. (1971). *The B book*. New York: Random House.
Enderle, J. R. (1994). *Six snowy sheep*. Hanesdale, PA: Boyds Mills Press.
Lipman, D. (1994). We *all go together: Creative activities for children to use with multicultural folksongs*. Phoenix, AZ: Oryx Press.
MacDonald, S. (1994). *Sea shapes*. San Diego: Gulliver Press, Harcourt Brace.
Massie, D. R. (2000). *The baby beebee bird*. New York: HarperCollins.
McLeod, E. (1975). *The bear's bicycle*. New York: Little Brown.
Numeroff, L. (1988). *If you give a moose a muffin*. New York: Scholastic.
O'Conner, J. (1997). *Benny's big bubble*. New York: Grosset.

Read With: Selections in This Book

Use these selections to introduce the sounds or to go on word hunts looking for words that start with the feature sounds.

Sort 1: *My Fruit*
Sort 2: *Circles*
Selection 1: *Baa, Baa, Black Sheep*
Selection 2: *Rain, Rain, Go Away*
Selection 3: *Old Mister Rabbit*
Sort 4: *Socks, Shoes, Caps, and Gloves*
Concept of Word Activities, Selection 1: *Rain on the Green Grass*
Concept of Word Activities, Selection 4: *My Family Sits on the Bed*
Concept of Word Activities, Selection 5: *Row, Row, Row Your Boat*

Demonstrate the Sort

Begin by contrasting *m* and *s* and introduce the letter pages. A few days later, introduce *b* and *r*. Then combine them all in a sort of four letters. Follow the directions above to demonstrate the beginning consonant sort and engage children in follow-up activities. The final sort of all four consonants will look something like this:

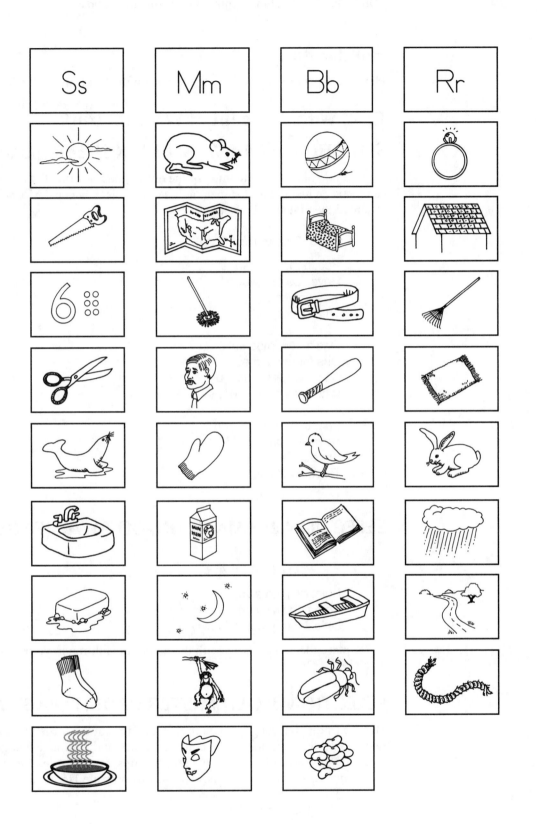

Handwriting

Have students practice writing the letters on the third row of the letter page.

Read With: Concept of Word in Print
SELECTION 1: *BAA, BAA, BLACK SHEEP* (page 112)

Children do not have to memorize the entire poem for practicing concept of word. You can focus on just the first stanza of "Baa, Baa, Black Sheep." Most children will be able to reread the first and third stanzas.

Baa, Baa, Black Sheep

Baa, baa, black sheep,
Have you any wool?
Yes sir, yes sir,
Three bags full.

One for my master,
One for my dame,
And one for the little boy
Who lives in the lane.

Baa, baa, black sheep,
Have you any wool?
Yes sir, yes sir,
Three bags full.

SELECTION 2: RAIN, RAIN, GO AWAY (PAGE 113)

Rain, Rain, Go Away

Rain, rain, go away,
Come again some other day.
Little Johnny wants to play.

Replace the name *Johnny* with the names of children in your class.

SELECTION 3: OLD MISTER RABBIT (PAGE 114)

This is a traditional song or chant that Doug Lipman describes in *We All Go Together*. The two ending lines are ideal for sentence frames and fill-ins. He suggests changing the food, and then changing where the rabbit jumps, for example, *"Of jumping in my kitchen, And eating our spaghetti."* Use the Word Cards on page 115 to rebuild the sentence.

Old Mister Rabbit

Old Mister Rabbit,
You've got a mighty habit,
Of jumping in my garden
And eating all my cabbage.

SORTS 18–20 PART II: BEGINNING CONSONANT SOUND SORTS FOR /T/, /G/, /N/, /P/

Notes for the Teacher

The next set of letter sounds are *t*, *g*, *n*, and *p*. They are introduced first as two separate sorts and then combined into one. These contrasts are straightforward for many students. Students should continue to practice the previous sorts.

Sounds Across Languages

Some students find the /g/ sound hard to pronounce and can confuse it with a /k/. This may be true for students who speak Arabic, French, or Swahili. The /t/ sound is often substituted for slightly more complex sounds like /th/. Some students may pronounce /p/ as /b/, and may substitute the /t/ for the /d/ sound. In many dialects of Chinese, students do not have a /n/ sound. This /n/ sound may be confused with /l/. For Spanish-speaking students, /p/ may sound like /b/, /t/ like /d/, and /k/ like /g/.

SORT 18 /T/, /G/ (pages 133 and 134)

SORT 19 /N/, /P/ (pages 135 and 136)

SORT 20 /T/, /G/, /N/, /P/ (pages 133–136)

Tt	Gg	Nn	Pp
toes	goat	nose	pig
tent	girl	nest	paint
top	gas	nut	pie
tub	gum	net	pen
tie	gate	9	pan
2	game	nails	pear
tube	goose	newspaper	pin
towel		needle	pail
turtle			

Read To: Literature Links

Calmenson, S. (2002). *The teeny tiny teacher*. New York: Scholastic.
Gibbons, G. (2001). *Gulls, gulls, gulls*. New York: Holiday House.
McPhail, D. (1996). *Pigs aplenty, pigs galore*. London: Puffin.

Read With: Selections in This Book

Selection 1: *Teddy Bear, Teddy Bear*
Selection 2: *Good Morning to You*
Selection 3: *Raining*
Sort 1: *My Fruit*
Concept of Word Activities, Selection 2: *Peas Porridge Hot*

SELECTION 1: TEDDY BEAR, TEDDY BEAR (page 116)

This is a jump rope rhyme that young students like to act out.

Teddy Bear, Teddy Bear

Teddy Bear, Teddy Bear, turn around.
Teddy Bear, Teddy Bear, touch the ground.
Teddy Bear, Teddy Bear, turn out the lights.
Teddy Bear, Teddy Bear, say, goodnight!

SELECTION 2: GOOD MORNING TO YOU (page 117)

Sing this selection to the tune of *Happy Birthday*. This is a cheerful song to sing as you come together in the morning. Students sing to a partner taking turns substituting their names.

Good Morning to You

Good Morning to you
Good Morning to you
Good Morning dear _____ (someone's name),
Good Morning to you.

SELECTION 3: RAINING

This traditional poem, on page 118, divides into two-line segments that make it easier for students to reread.

A rhyming picture sort, sentence strips for the first four lines, and words to match to the strips are presented in a blackline master.

Raining

It's raining, it's pouring,
The old man is snoring.

He went to bed and bumped his head,
And couldn't get up in the morning.

SORTS 21-23   BEGINNING CONSONANT SOUND SORTS FOR /C/, /H/, /F/, /D/

Notes for the Teacher

The letter *c* is introduced as a hard sound, /k/, so expect some confusion as children hunt for words that begin with *c*. You can explain that students are correct when they want to say that the letter *c* makes a /s/ sound. You can create a separate category for such pictures: "I put the word *circle* over here, because, yes, it has the letter *c* at the beginning, but it has an /sss/ sound like the word *sun*." When asked to think of words that begin with *c*, students may think of words that begin with the letter *k*. You can tell them about words that sound the same but begin with a different letter. For example, "Kate's name begins with a *k*, and it sounds the same as the beginning of *cake*, which begins with a *c*."

By this time, students are familiar with routines that extend their study of these sounds.

Sounds Across Languages

These common beginning sounds and letters in English are easily confused with similar sounds by students from other language backgrounds. Some students may confuse the hard sound of *c*, /k/, with the /g/ sound and may pronounce *cat* as *gat*. In some languages, the *c* is pronounced as a soft sound like /s/, as it is in many English words (*circle*, *center*).

The /h/ sound is different for Spanish and Chinese speakers than in English, and can be difficult to pronounce in a standard form; in Spanish, *h* is silent, and in Chinese the sound for /h/ may sound more like /kh/ as in *loch*. In Arabic, /f/ may be substituted for /v/, and /d/ for the *th* sound in *this*. In Japanese, the /f/ sound may be pronounced /h/ (*han* for *fan*).

Also in Spanish, the /d/ sound is pronounced as the *th* sound in *this*, and a word like *dog* may be pronounced *thog*. Listen for how students pronounce the beginning sound, and look for change over time. For the time being, the letter *d* may be associated with the /th/ sound. This association is acceptable while students learn more about the pronunciation of standard English.

SORT 21 /C/, /H/ (pages 137 and 138)
SORT 22 /F/, /D/ (pages 139 and 140)
SORT 23 /C/, /H/, /F/, /D/ (pages 137–140)

Cc	Hh	Ff	Dd
cat	hand	fish	dog
cup	horse	5	deer
cow	house	fork	doll
cake	hose	fence	duck
coat	horn	fan	door
car	hook	foot	dice
candle	heart	fox	desk
can	hat	fire	dive
comb	ham	4	dishes

Read To: Literature Links

Dr. Seuss. (1968). *The foot book*. New York: Random House.
Perkins, A. (1969). *Hand, hand, fingers, thumb*. New York: Random House.

Read With: Selections in this Book

Selection 1: *Hop a Little, Jump a Little*
Selection 2: *Hickory Dickory Dock*
Selection 3: *Pat a Cake, Pat a Cake*
Sort 1: *My Fruit*
Concept of Word Activities, Selection 7: *Happy Birthday*
Concept of Word Activities, Section 15: *Humpty Dumpty*

SELECTION 1: HOP A LITTLE, JUMP A LITTLE (page 120)

The two-syllable word "little" calls for careful tracking when students reread this piece.

Hop a Little, Jump a Little

Hop a little, jump a little,
    One, two, three;
Run a little, skip a little,
    Tap one knee;
Bend a little, stretch a little,
    Nod your head;
Yawn a little, sleep a little,
    In your bed.

SELECTION 2: HICKORY DICKORY DOCK (page 121)

Many children will know this familiar rhyme. Recite it together before you show the printed form on page 121. Talk about grandfather clocks and show a picture (perhaps from a nursery rhyme collection) so children will understand how a mouse might run up and down a clock.

Hickory Dickory Dock

Hickory dickory dock,
The mouse ran up the clock!
The clock struck one.
The mouse ran down.
Hickory dickory dock.

SELECTION 3: PAT A CAKE, PAT A CAKE (page 122)

This selection emphasizes the /k/ sound with *cake*. It is also a good place to review a number of other letters and sounds.

Children enjoy pantomiming these actions. They pat the dough and enjoy substituting their own letters for the B. One student opens the door to the pretend oven while the other extends arms to place the tray inside. Students substitute the first letter of their partner's name for *B*, and their partner's name for *baby*: "*Mark it with a P . . . for Pedro and me.*"

Pat a Cake, Pat a Cake

Pat a cake, pat a cake, baker's man!
Bake me a cake as fast as you can,
Pat it, and dot it, and mark it with a B,
And put it in the oven
For baby and me.

SORTS 24–27   BEGINNING CONSONANT SOUND SORTS FOR /L/,/K/,/J/,/W/, /Y/,/Z/, /V/

Notes for the Teacher

These sounds are a little harder to pronounce, and are lower-frequency letters, as indicated by how few pages of these letters there are in English dictionaries.

Sounds Across Languages

Spanish-speaking students may pronounce the /k/ sound more like a /g/ (*gangaroo* for *kangaroo*). Because of Spanish words like *jalapeño* or *José*, students may pronounce English words that begin with a *j* with a /kh/ or /h/ sound. /z/ may sound like /s/ and /v/ may be pronounced /b/. The /y/ sound in English may be pronounced like /ch/ (*you* as *chew*). The /w/ sound may be pronounced with more of a /gw/ sound; *when* may be spelled GUEN.

The /v/ sound is confused in a number of languages. In Chinese there is no /v/; /w/ and /f/ are substituted for the /v/. In other languages, the /v/ may be pronounced as /b/, as in Korean, or as /f/, as in Thai. As noted for the /s/ sound, /s/ may be substituted for /z/.

SORT 24 /L/,/K/ (pages 141 and 142)
SORT 25 /J/,/W/ (pages 143 and 144)
SORT 26 /L/,/K/,/J/,/W/ (pages 141–144)
SORT 27 /Y/,/Z/,/V/ (pages 145–147)

L l	K k	J j	W w
lamp	key	jug	watch
leaf	king	jet	web
log	kitchen	jar	worm
lock	kite	jacket	witch
letter	kick	jump	wig
leg	kitten	jeep	wall
lip	kangaroo	jacks	wing
		jog	well
			window

Y y	Z z	V v
yarn	zipper	van
yo-yo	zebra	vine
yolk	zero	vacuum
yawn	zoo	vest
yogurt	zig-zag	vase
yard		volcano
yell		violin
		valentine

Read To: Literature Links

Kalen, R. (1989). *Jump, frog, jump!* New York: HarperTrophy.

Read With: Selections in This Book

Selection 1: *Lollipops*
Selection 2: *Soft Kitty*
Selection 3: *Jack and Jill*

Selection 4: *Fuzzy Wuzzy*
Selection 5: *Valentines*
Selection 6: *Train is a Coming, Oh Yeh*
Sort 1, *My Fruit*
Concept of Word Activities, Selection 3: *Jump Rope, Jump Rope*

Read With: Concept of Word in Print

SELECTION 1: LOLLIPOPS (page 123)

This poem is ideal for syllabication and for finding the three *l*s inside *Lollipops*. Have students pretend to lick the lollipop in cadence with *"Lick, lick, lick."*

Lollipops

Lollipops, lollipops,
Lick, lick, lick.
Lollipops, lollipops,
Good on the stick.

SELECTION 2: SOFT KITTY (page 124)

Soft Kitty

Soft kitty, warm kitty,
Little ball of fur.
Sleepy kitty, happy kitty,
Purr, purr, purrrrrrrr.

SELECTION 3: JACK AND JILL (page 125)

Students move their fingers walking up the hill and tumbling down as they recite the rhyme. A concept sort can be created of things that you would find outside (on the hill) and things you would find inside (where Jack is laid up after his accident).

Jack and Jill

Jack and Jill went up the hill
To fetch a pail of water.
Jack fell down
And broke his crown.
And Jill came tumbling after.

SELECTION 4: FUZZY WUZZY (page 126)

Find the *z*s in this poem. Reciting this favorite tickles as the *z*s vibrate.

Fuzzy Wuzzy

Fuzzy Wuzzy
was a bear,
Fuzzy Wuzzy
had no hair,
Fuzzy Wuzzy
wasn't really fuzzy,
Was he?

SELECTION 5: VALENTINES (page 127)

Valentines

Valentines Red
Valentines Blue
This valentine says
"I love you."

SELECTION 6: TRAIN IS A COMING, OH YEH (page 128)

The repetition of the phrase *"oh yeh"* delights the students, who enjoy emphasizing *yeh*. We ask, "What other words do you know that sound like *yeh* at the beginning?" Doug Lipman in *We All Go Together* first introduced us to this traditional song. There are several new vocabulary terms in this song about trains. Reread just one or two of your students' favorite stanzas.

Students can learn about trains as they pantomime the different activities. To act like engineers have students pull back on the throttle and whistle: *"The throttle tells the train how fast to go."* The conductor punches the tickets. Students pretend to join the train as cars as they sing and train around the room.

Train is a Coming, Oh Yeh

Train is a coming, oh yeh,
Train is a coming,
Train is a coming,
Train is a coming, oh yeh.

You better get your ticket, oh yeh,
You better get your ticket,
You better get your ticket,
You better get your ticket, oh yeh.

Whistle is a-blowing, oh yeh,
Whistle is a-blowing,
Whistle is a-blowing,
Whistle is a-blowing, oh yeh.

Train is going home now, oh yeh,
Train is going home now,
Train is going home now,
Train is going home now, oh yeh.

Name _____   Date/Story Number_____

Baa, Baa, Black Sheep

Baa, baa, black sheep,
Have you any wool?
Yes sir, yes sir,
Three bags full.

One for my master,
One for my dame,
And one for the little boy
Who lives in the lane.

Baa, baa, black sheep,
Have you any wool?
Yes sir, yes sir,
Three bags full.

Name _____   Date/Story Number_____

Rain, Rain, Go Away

Rain, rain, go away,

Come again some other day.

Little Johnny wants to play.

Name_____   Date/Story Number_____

Old Mister Rabbit

Old Mister Rabbit,

You've got a mighty habit,

Of jumping in my garden

And eating all my cabbage.

Old Mister Rabbit, You've got a mighty habit,

Old	Mister
got	a

Rabbit	You've
mighty	habit

Words Their Way: Letter and Picture Sorts for Emergent Spellers © 2006 by Prentice-Hall, Inc.

Name_____   Date/Story Number_____

Teddy Bear, Teddy Bear

Teddy Bear, Teddy Bear,
  turn around.

Teddy Bear, Teddy Bear,
  touch the ground.

Teddy Bear, Teddy Bear,
  turn out the lights.

Teddy Bear, Teddy Bear,
  say, goodnight!

Name_____   Date/Story Number_____

Good Morning to You

Good morning to you

Good morning to you

Good morning dear _____

Good morning to you.

Name _____   Date/Story Number_____

Raining

It's raining, it's pouring,

The old man is snoring.

He went to bed and bumped his head,

And couldn't get up in the morning.

Words Their Way: Letter and Picture Sorts for Emergent Spellers © 2006 by Prentice-Hall, Inc.

It's raining, it's pouring, The old man is snoring.

		it's
raining		old
		snoring.
It's	the	is
pouring		man

Name_____   Date/Story Number_____

Hop a Little, Jump a Little

Hop a little, jump a little,

One, two, three;

Run a little, skip a little,

Tap one knee;

Bend a little, stretch a little,

Nod your head;

Yawn a little, sleep a little,

In your bed.

Words Their Way: Letter and Picture Sorts for Emergent Spellers © 2006 by Prentice-Hall, Inc.

Number_____   Date/Story Number_____

Hickory Dickory Dock

Hickory dickory dock,

The mouse ran up the clock!

The clock struck one.

The mouse ran down.

Hickory dickory dock.

Name_____   Date/Story Number_____

Pat a Cake, Pat a Cake

Pat a cake, pat a cake, baker's man!

Bake me a cake as fast as you can,

Pat it, and dot it, and mark it with a B,

And put it in the oven

For baby and me.

Words Their Way: Letter and Picture Sorts for Emergent Spellers © 2006 by Prentice-Hall, Inc.

Name_____   Date/Story Number_____

Lollipops

Lollipops, lollipops,

Lick, lick, lick.

Lollipops, lollipops,

Good on the stick.

Name_____   Date/Story Number_____

Soft Kitty

Soft kitty, warm kitty,

Little ball of fur.

Sleepy kitty, happy kitty,

Purr, purr, purrrrrrrr.

Words Their Way: Letter and Picture Sorts for Emergent Spellers © 2006 by Prentice-Hall, Inc.

Name _____   Date/Story Number_____

Jack and Jill

Jack and Jill went up the hill

To fetch a pail of water.

Jack fell down

And broke his crown.

And Jill came tumbling after.

Name _____   Date/Story Number_____

Fuzzy Wuzzy

Fuzzy Wuzzy

was a bear,

Fuzzy Wuzzy

had no hair,

Fuzzy Wuzzy

wasn't really fuzzy,

Was he?

Name_____   Date/Story Number_____

Valentines

Valentines red

Valentines blue

This valentine says

"I love you."

Name_____   Date/Story Number_____

Train is a Coming, Oh Yeh

Train is a coming, oh yeh,
Train is a coming,
Train is a coming,
Train is a coming, oh yeh.

You better get your ticket, oh yeh,
You better get your ticket,
You better get your ticket,
You better get your ticket, oh yeh.

Whistle is a-blowing, oh yeh,
Whistle is a-blowing,
Whistle is a-blowing,
Whistle is a-blowing, oh yeh.

Train is going home now, oh yeh,
Train is going home now,
Train is going home now,
Train is going home now, oh yeh.

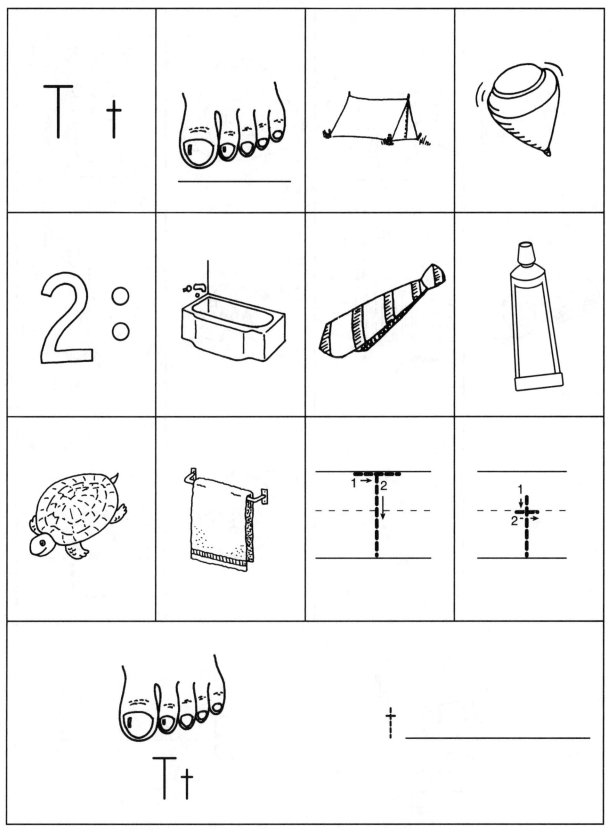

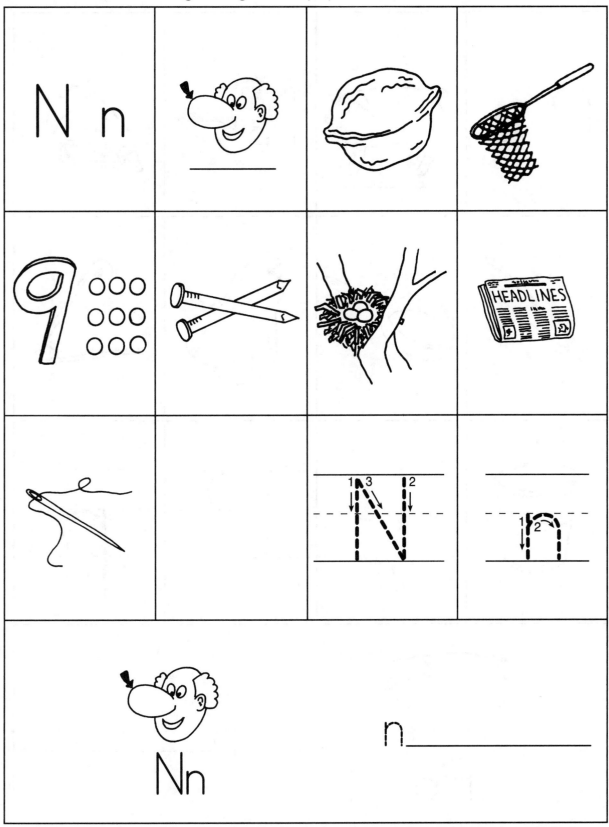

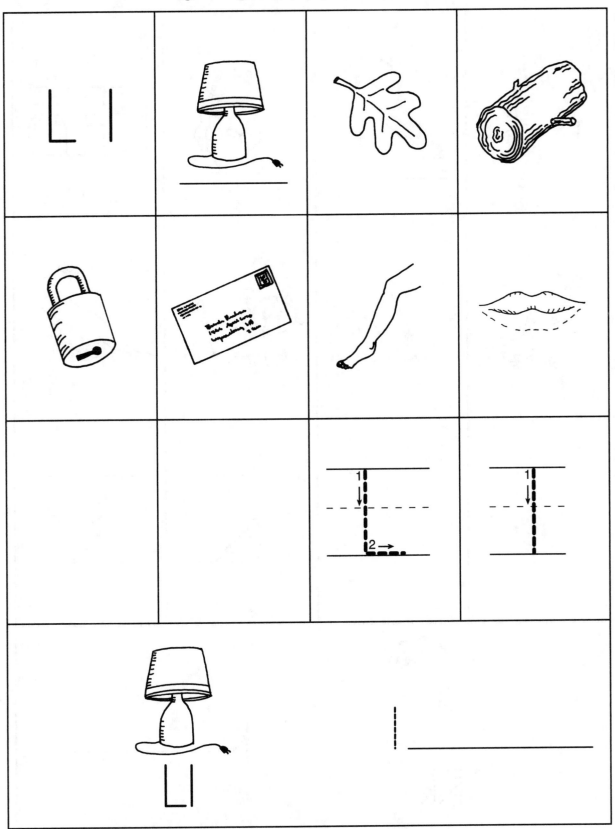

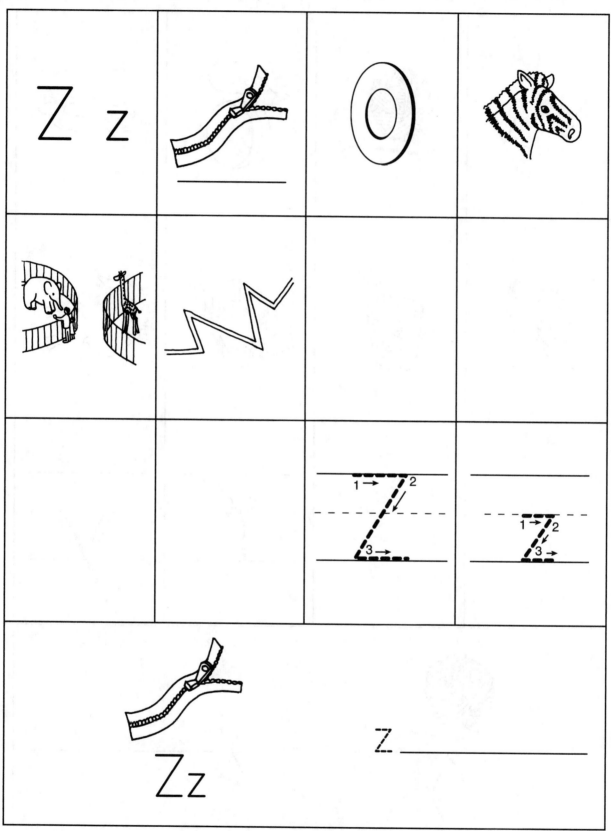

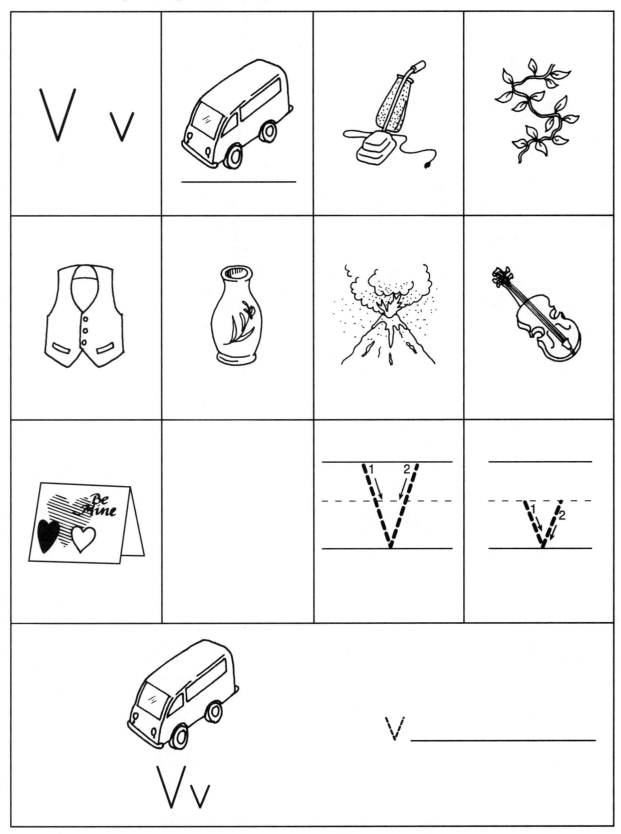

ASSESSMENT OF

The Emergent Stage

At the end of kindergarten, the *Kindergarten Spelling Inventory* in *Words Their Way* and the Concept of Word measure here are key assessments. We provide some assessment forms, but much of the assessment is done in the course of daily teaching.

READ WITH: CONCEPT OF WORD IN PRINT

Return to *Humpty Dumpty* introduced in the Concept of Word in Print Activities on page 79. Assess concept of word work with one child at a time. Observe how well the child can track, using the checklist on page 74. Ask the child to find words in context and then assess sight word learning by asking the child to read the list of words on page 151.

Benchmarks:

_____ *Fingerpoint Reading.* Model fingerpoint reading and ask students to fingerpoint read. At the end of kindergarten, the benchmark is for students to read **all 5 lines** accurately.

_____ *Word Identification in Context.* Point to the underlined words in *Humpty Dumpty* or *Me Levanto* and ask: "*What word is this?*" At the end of kindergarten, students correctly identify **9 out of 10** words in context.

_____ *Words in Isolation.* Show a student the list of words from the following blackline. Say: "*Put your finger next to the first word. Tell me the words that you know.*" Count how many sight words they are able to recall. At the end of kindergarten, students read **7 of the 10** words correctly.

Word list from *Humpty Dumpty*:

_____ on		_____ men	
_____ Humpty		_____ king's	
_____ put		_____ wall	
_____ horses		_____ had	
_____ sat		_____ fall	

SPANISH READ WITH: CONCEPT OF WORD IN PRINT

Here is a poem that we have used for Spanish speakers to observe concept of word.

Me Levanto

Yo me levanto
   Muy de mañana.
Cuando el sol entra
   Por mi ventana.

LOWERCASE ALPHABET RECOGNITION ASSESSMENT

You can conduct this assessment individually or in a small group. Give each student a copy of the Alphabet Recognition Assessment. Alphabet knowledge of capital letters was assessed in sort 4 (page 17) and should be repeated as needed.

A global view of students' alphabet knowledge is observed when each student has a copy of the Alphabet Recognition Assessment. Following the directions just noted, observe as students read the letters aloud to themselves or a partner. Early emergent students will repeat the names of a few letters that they know. Late emergent learners will read the letters accurately at a faster pace.

Instructions for Assessment of Individuals: As each child points and names, record their responses on a copy of the form. If a child identifies *l* as *"one"* ask the student what letter it could be. *"Put your finger on each letter and say the name of the letter. Skip the letter if you do not know the name of the letter."*

According to PALS benchmarks, at the end of kindergarten, students on average know the names of 24 of the 26 lowercase letters. The time it takes students to name the letters with benchmark accuracy may range from 20–40 seconds.

ASSESSMENT OF BEGINNING CONSONANTS

A spelling inventory, such as the *Kindergarten Spelling Inventory* in the Appendix of *Words Their Way*, can be administered in small groups to determine whether children are using consonants. Two other ways to assess consonants are included here. A score of 12 is the benchmark for the end of kindergarten. The *Emergent Class Record*, also in the Appendix of *Words Their Way*, is a summary sheet of students' progress used to organize instruction.

ASSESSMENT FOR BEGINNING SOUNDS

Instructions: Make a copy of the assessment on page 153 for each student. You can conduct this individually or in small groups. Explain: "Put your finger on the sun. Say the word *sun*. What picture sounds like *sun* at the beginning: *book, soap, jet*? Circle the soap because *sssun* and *sssoap* begin the same." Continue, without giving feedback or emphasizing the sounds at the beginning of the words. Name the pictures for students to be sure they use the right labels and guide them in the completion of this assessment.

Benchmark: Students at the end of kindergarten complete **7 out of 8** correctly.

*	sun	book	**soap**	jet
1.	nose	fan	kite	**nine**
2.	rabbit	**rug**	dog	leaf
3.	lamp	cat	toe	**log**
4.	watch	**web**	zero	van
5.	belt	kitty	yo-yo	**bird**
6.	pie	**pig**	ball	gum
7.	zebra	key	**zip**	hand
8.	dog	jet	leaf	**desk**